THE HOLY FAMILY OF FATHER MOON

Joseph H. Fichter

LEAVEN PRESS

Library of Congress Catalog Card Number:
    ISBN: 0-934134-13-8
Published by: Leaven Press
                     P.O. Box 40292
                     Kansas City, MO 64141

Printed and bound in the United States of America

Contents

Introduction

If this were a book about the Charismatic renewal in the Catholic Church I would probably not be asked by some conventional clergyman, "How did you ever get mixed up with those people?" If I proposed a year-long study of the *Opus Dei* movement, no fellow sociologist would ask whether I am receiving large stipends and enjoying all-expense-paid trips to conventions. Even if I decided to study the Baptist foreign mission work in South America, I would hardly be told that I am lending an aura of academic prestige to an odd religious activity. In other words, I would not feel the need to explain my motives for such studies except to say that I am a typical sociologist interested in the group behavior of religious people.

Researching the Unification Church seems to require an academic apology. Since the church is the target of religious bigotry and the object of attack in the news media it is said to besmirch the reputation of any scholar or clergyman who takes it seriously and who consorts with its leaders. When I attended the seventh annual International Conference on the Unity of Science (ICUS) in San Francisco pickets were carrying anti-Moon placards outside the Fairmont Hotel. This happened again the following year at the Boston Sheraton. A more personal reprimand came from a New England professor who accepted the hospitality of the Moonies—roundtrip airfare and three days lodging and meals—for the ninth ICUS at the Fontainbleau Hotel in Miami Beach. He later wrote to all academic participants, warning them against the evils of Mr. Moon, admitting that he had surreptitiously accepted this benefice in order to seek out his son, whom he later kidnapped and deprogrammed.[1] Professor Douglas Lenz piously proclaimed it reprehensible that a Catholic scholar and clergyman lends his presence to the Moonie enterprise.

1

Another scolding came from the Jesuit editor of *Etude* in Paris, whose protegé, a young Jesuit seminarian, had left the order to join the Moonies. At the same time two former diocesan seminarians also became active in the French Unification Church. In early May 1981, a complaint was lodged against me with Jesuit headquarters in Rome, concerning the French version of my *America* article on the Moonies.[2] This article also raised the ire of two French Catholic laymen, one whose daughter had joined the Moonies eight years previously and was then in the United States. He begged me to use my influence with the Unification leaders to release her from captivity. There were also several enquiries from Germany after the German version had appeared in *Neue Hoffnung*.

One of the more arrogant observations sometimes heard among academics is that a college professor who associates with the Unification Church "bestows respectability" on a movement that is not respectable. On the other hand, one hears from some clergymen that you "lend credence" to an obviously heretical movement by attending Moonie conferences and symposia where theological questions are discussed. Lay people, especially churchgoers, profess to be scandalized that a Catholic priest will defend the civil rights of people who deny the divinity of Christ and who "arrange marriages" for their young members. Running through all these complaints and comments is the popular calumny that the young Moonies are deceived, brainwashed and held virtual prisoners to the cult.

American history provides some sad examples of bigotry, hatred and discrimination against religious minorities, and we are witnessing now a renewal of such mindless antagonism against the Unification Church. We generally pride ourselves on American fairness and religious tolerance which seem, however, to be applicable only among the conventional mainline religions. Since the Second Vatican Council Catholics, whose ancestors were the victims of religious discrimination, now have renewed motivation to behave ecumenically toward other religious groups, including even the strange cults recently appearing on the American scene.

My first knowledge of the Moonies came from a study John Lofland did on the West Coast in 1965 of a small group of pious people he called the "Doomsday Cult." He still refuses to say that these were the early American Moonies. Even though his "pseudonyms are now somewhat labored" he insists that he "must continue to protect the anonymity of the movement." Herbert Richardson almost "blows his cover" when he says that "Lofland's earlier work [was] widely assumed to have been done on the beginnings in this country of the Unification Church of Reverend Moon."[3] In the early 1960s Lofland saw little future for this "obscure end-of-the-world religion" which he belittled as a "small and laughable bunch of kooks." The spectacular growth of the "Divine Precepts" in the next decade called for an explanation he provided in the epilogue of the enlarged edition of 1977.[4] Even then he doubted its further growth.

Other scholars recognized the more permanent quality of the Unification movement and began to take serious notice of the church and its founder, Reverend Sun Myung Moon. One of these is Professor Frederick Sontag, of the Department of Philosophy at Pomona College, who visited most of the church centers, interviewed many leaders and members, and authored a well-balanced and objective report.[5] Even before this book was published in 1977 I had read a torrent of derogatory articles and stories about the Unification movement, and had also completed a research report on a Catholic "cult," the Pentecostal renewal.[6] My curiosity was further aroused when I received and accepted invitations to conferences on Unification ideology at Acapulco and San Juan, Puerto Rico.

This book is a sociological analysis of the main structural features of the Unification Church and is probably best listed in the academic discipline of ecclesiology. Most of its content has been well rehearsed, has emerged from lectures and articles I delivered, and conversations, discussions and symposia in which I have participated. It seems to me that this explanatory introduction is helpful in describing my motivations for being involved with this religious movement and also in raising some intriguing theological questions. I had frequent personal contact with Moonies and it was this experience, more than the literature of the movement, that attracted my sociological attention.

Aside from the typical curiosity of the social researcher that I wanted to satisfy in the pursuit of this study, I have two objective reasons for making a study of the Moonies. The first is my deep desire to promote the ecumenical outreach which has been a modern feature of the Catholic Church since the Second Vatican Council. This I see as an obligation for the fully committed religious believer. The second motive is my concern about the prevalent religious bigotry that is being expressed against the so-called "cults," the new religious movements, especially the Unification Church. To replace bigotry with tolerance and ignorance with information seems a worthy objective in a democratic society.

Footnotes

1   See the story told by his son, Douglas Lenz, "Twenty-Two Months as a Moonie," *LCA Partners,* February 1982, pp. 12-15
2   See "Marriage, Family and Sun Myung Moon," *America,* October 27, 1979, pp. 226-228
3   James T. Richardson, ed., *Conversion Careers,* Beverly Hills, Sage, 1978, p. 10, with reference to John Lofland, *Doomsday Cult,* Englewood Cliffs, Prentice-Hall, 1966
4   The enlarged edition was reissued in 1981 by Irvington Publishers with the epilogue, pp. 279-344, "The Boom and Bust of a Millenarian Movement: Doomsday Cult Revisited"
5   Frederick Sontag, *Sun Myung Moon and the Unification Church,* Nashville, Abingdon, 1977. His bibliography, pp. 217-224, lists all available books and articles on the movement to that date.
6   Joseph H. Fichter, *The Catholic Cult of the Paraclete,* New York, Sheed and Ward, 1975

I Religious Cults Under Attack

We Americans like to congratulate ourselves that we have learned to live comfortably and at peace in a pluralistic religious society. As early as 1908 the *Christian Century* rejoiced that the denominations were "cultivating a spirit of fellowship and cooperation across sectarian lines. They have organized what they call a Federation of Churches—a scheme to cooperate yet further and on a large scale." After all these years Alvin Illig writes that "under the impulse of the Holy Spirit the chemistry of ecumenism is preparing the Christian community for collaboration in evangelization, turning distrust into trust, suspicion into respect, competition into cooperation." Recent large interchurch happenings underscore this interpretation. Lutherans and Episcopalians have agreed to intercommunion; three large Lutheran congregations have decided to incorporate into a single church. Southern Presbyterians have joined up with United Presbyterians. We have become increasingly tolerant of major denominational differences. No more Salem witch hunts. No killing of Mormons and Quakers. No Nativist attacks against Catholics and Jews. The Gallup pollsters found that 73% of Protestants are favorable to the Catholic community, while 87% of Catholics today look favorably on their Protestant brothers and sisters.

Unholy Alliance

While we bask in this aura of happy ecumenism and religious sophistication, many of us seem unaware that a new and subtle wave of bigotry is sweeping the country, promoted by prelates and priests, by judges and legislators, by editors, journalists and newscasters, and by parents of young people who convert to any of the so-called "new" religions. There appears to be an almost systematic program of defamation of groups like Hare Krishnas, Children of God, the Unification Church, the Forever Family, and The Way. These were specifically singled out for a warning by the General Secretary of the United States Catholic Conference in a letter to the American bishops. He said that "the rise and propagation of various kinds of religious and semi-religious cults has been a growing phenomenon in the United States over the last decade or more."[1] This letter was careful not to attack or condemn the cults, but it included a brochure, "Cults and Kids," which did so.

This kind of polite warning by one Catholic bishop was expanded to a collective condemnation of the cults after the mass wedding of 2,042 Moonie couples at Madison Square Garden. The *New York Times* headlined the news: "Major Faiths in City Undertaking First Unified Effort Against Cults." We read that Jews, Catholics and Protestants "have joined together this summer for the first time to combat what they call 'destructive cults,' mentioning in particular the Unification Church of the Reverend Sun Myung Moon." We have here an unholy alliance, publicly endorsed by prominent religious leaders, to conduct a deliberate religious persecution.[2]

Slander is irreligious, kidnapping is criminal, deprogramming is unconstitutional, but the most frightening attack now by the anti-cultists is the insistence that religious conversion is a new kind of mental illness. If you are a political dissident in Russia you are judged mentally sick and locked up in an insane asylum. Among the anti-cultists, if you are a religious dissident you suffer a mental sickness called "Snapping," a sudden personality change. The convert must be captured, physically restrained and psychologically coerced until he or she snaps back to a normal American secular way of thinking and living.[3]

During the past two decades many changes have occurred on the American religious scene, but the direction of change and the response to new religious developments have not always been anticipated by either religionists or sociologists. Some religious innovations are acceptable, and others are not. Who would have predicted that the new religious youth movements would be so widely condemned? We say that we are pluralistic in religion, but in a subtle way we are also saying that there are limits to the kinds of religion we will tolerate.

The problem raised by Bishop Kelly and the interfaith crusade against the Moonies provoke a series of questions that I would like to discuss further: (a) What is the nature of the contemporary religious revival? (b) What is so different about the religious youth movements? (c) Are the cults really destructive and dangerous? (d) What reasons do we give for our bigotry? (e) Is there an intelligent Christian response?

Rebirth of American Religion

It is not so long ago that Harvey Cox declared that the process of secularization is "almost certainly irreversible."[4] More recently, Peter Berger said just about the opposite: "The most obvious fact about the contemporary world is not so much its secularity, but rather its great hunger for redemption and transcendence."[5] An international survey, commissioned by the Center for Applied Research in the Apostolate (CARA), found that religious belief and practice are stronger in the United States than in most other countries of the world.[6] Large proportions of Americans believe in God and in the afterlife, say prayers and attend worship services. Gallup reported that 69% believe in the divinity of Christ. Increasing numbers take the spiritual life seriously, and a significant minority have had a spiritual "experience." More than one-third claim they have been religiously "born again."

Aside from these general statistics about religious beliefs and behavior of the American people, the most spectacular evidences of religious revival are at two age levels: young, innovative and enthusiastic Americans are expressing their religion in a variety of cultic movements. Conservative and middle-aged Americans have begun to place great faith in the so-called "moral majority," which is a cultic movement of its own, with a membership crosscutting most of the larger denominations.

The spiritual message for religious conversion reaches the largest number of Americans through the airwaves of communication. The 50,000-watt clear-channel radio station owned by Loyola University in New Orleans has a waiting list of preachers who want to buy time, including the prime hours of the evening, to deliver their message. The rising power of the televangelists is well documented by Jeffrey Hadden and Charles Swann, who report that 66 syndicated programs in 1980 reached a combined audience of over 20,000,000 viewers.[7]

The call to repentance and to a religious awakening is being experienced also outside the regular Sunday morning hours of worship (at home and at church), especially in the Spirituality Centers that have been established on the grounds of former seminaries and semi-abandoned monasteries. These and the traditional retreat houses, run by religious congregations, both male and female, are attracting increasingly large crowds of retreatants. Attendance records are broken each year as more and more lay people search for whatever benefits they anticipate from prayer, meditation, silence, and scripture reading.

A non-religious system of "centering meditation" has been successfully marketed by Ira Progoff under the name of *Intensive Journal* (trademark registered). Thousands of Americans are flocking to the workshops that explain this method and to the "retreats" that present the process under the sponsorship of religious facilities and under the direction of clergy and religious women.[8] The Progoff process is similar to the quietist kind of transcendental meditation long associated with the mystics of the Christian tradition and of the East.

The turn to Eastern religions has attracted growing numbers of young Americans from the fairly educated middle class who are not hippies or doped-up dropouts. Some of these groups are called "new" religions only because they are new to the conventional Christians of this country. Hinduism, Buddhism, Sufism, Zen, Baba-lovers, Subud, Siddha Yoga are presented and promoted by numerous and various swamis, gurus and spiritual masters.

Spiritual rebirth of Americans, however, is not the exclusive pro-

duct of Eastern swamis, a fact clearly demonstrated in the unexpected mushrooming of the Catholic charismatic movement. This
cult of the Paraclete came almost suddenly on the American scene at
Duquesne University in 1967. It has remained firmly within the
Catholic Church instead of forming sectarian groups. This movement is reaching ecumenically into other suburban middle-class
churches.[9]

From a numerical point of view the quantitative growth of religion
in America is most noticeable in the old-time conservative, evangelical and fundamentalist churches. The so-called "fringe sects," identified by Henry van Dusen and analyzed by William McLaughlin,
were called the "Third Force in American Christendom," somewhere
between Catholicism and Protestantism. Dean Kelley's book, *Why
Conservative Churches Are Growing,* called attention to the strict
fundamentalist and exclusive sects that were far from liberal and
ecumenical: the Jehovah's Witnesses, Latter-Day Saints, Seventh
Day Adventists, Assemblies of God.[10]

In a comparative and competitive perspective we must note that
the contemporary religious revival has been an uneven movement.
While a remarkable growth occurred in the fundamentalist moral
majority and the conservative sects and enthusiastic cults, there has
been relatively little growth in the mainline churches, including
Catholicism.

What's Different About the Cults?

The sociological understanding of the cult derives from the concept of mysticism discussed by Ernst Troeltsch as a sociological
category distinct from sect and church.[11] It has been elaborated to
signify a new and syncretistic religious movement in its early stages,
and Geoffrey Nelson suggests that "all founded religions can be seen
as having developed from cults."[12] Most often the cult is now described as a small, informal, loosely structured, spontaneous group
clustered around a charismatic leader. In the theological and ritual
traditions of the Christian Church the cult was a group (and its

behavior) identified with a special devotion to a holy object, as the Sacred Heart of Jesus, the Virgin Mary, and any of the saints.

From this perspective one may say that the small group of Jesus' original followers constituted a Jewish cult that evolved over time into a sect, a denomination, and finally a church. The cult of mendicant religious poverty formed around Francis of Assisi and developed into a large religious brotherhood.

In our own times these meanings have changed, and in the ordinary language of the day, any religious group that is strange and exotic, deviant and different, is popularly called a cult. Back in the Great Depression there was a voodoo cult in New Orleans; the Kingdom of Father Divine flourished among northern urban blacks, and the Nation of Islam established mosques all over the country.[13] The first sociological study of the American Moonies by John Lofland was called *The Doomsday Cult*.[14] All of these groups were a little odd, not quite acceptable to conventional American churchgoers. In his testimony at the Dole hearings at Washington in 1979, Dean Kelley said cult "is a term that is usually used in a derogatory sense to apply to religions we don't understand and don't like."

The modern phenomenon about which so many middle-class American parents and clergy are concerned got its start in the youth turmoil of the 1960s when the dropouts, the hippies and flower children, who were not basically religious, were recruited to the fast-growing Jesus Movement. This development is seen by some as the death of the rebellious student movement, and by others as the start of a new American religious revival. The movement took many forms and spawned different expressions of the Jesus cults.

Among the many offshoots of the Jesus Movement, the cult that attracted the most and earliest notoriety was the Children of God, founded by David Berg in 1968 and spreading through the nation. The first abduction from any of the cults came when Ted Patrick forcibly kidnapped a member of the Children of God from their commune in Denver. In that same year, 1971, the first formal anti-cult movement was organized by a couple who could not persuade their daughter to leave the Children of God, and the term "deprogramming" was coined. This process is described as "abducting and detaining members of 'cults' against their will, haranguing them for extended periods of time under emotionally charged conditions, and then achieving in such individuals rapid redefinitions of their former religious experiences and beliefs that culminate in their apostasy."[15] Other new religions were also attracting young members whose parents objected vigorously to their membership in strange cults, especially to the Unification Church under the direction of Sun Myung Moon. This Korean missionary and evangelist had been preceded by zealous disciples who enlisted converts and prepared the way for Moon's nationwide tours in 1971 and 1972. The news media provided typically sensational coverage of the Moon rallies and helped to feed the fears of the anti-cultists. The newly established vigilantes formed chapters in various parts of the country, but with no interference from police, courts and judges. Public officials did not at first recognize the criminal character of the abductions and brainwashing by these vigilantes who established the Freedom of Thought Foundation with an isolated ranch in Arizona for the "rehabilitation" of kidnapped cult members.

It should be noted, however, that many parents of cult members do allow their children to make their own decisions about religious participation and accept gracefully the fact that the young people have converted to a different vocation. Those who were at first puzzled, or resentful, about their children's adherence to a new religion tended to make reasonable and loving adjustment to their changed parent-child relationship.

Are the Religious Cults Destructive?

After the initial spurt of criminal activity in kidnapping and deprogramming, the anti-cult movement began to flounder in disorganization and lack of competent leadership. Then came the tragic events at Jonestown in November, 1978, which served to revitalize the general antagonism to religious cults. As Enroth wrote in a less than objective style, "Since Jonestown the word 'cult' has assumed new significance on the American scene. In countless articles, interviews and editorial pages, the public has been made aware of the reality and destructive potential of religious-political groups that manipulate the mind, subvert the will, and vandalize the soul."[16] The pejorative concept of the cult was then fixed in the popular mind by the news media's lurid accounts of the final tragedy of Reverend Jim Jones and his People's Temple. "Perhaps, as John Hall suggested, journalists used the cult terminology in the hope that a label would suffice where an explanation was unavailable."[17]

While scholars and religionists and serious commentators struggled to understand the mass suicide of 912 church members in Guyana, the anti-cultists used it as a demonstration that their repeated fears of the new religious cults were well founded. Shortly thereafter Ted Patrick, the inventor of deprogramming, asserted that similar destructive tendencies existed in other religious groups like Scientology, Hare Krishnas and the Unification Church. He predicted in a *Playboy* interview in 1979 that the Jonestown disaster would spread "like wildfire" in all the other cults in America.[18] The potential for "mass suicide" was built into groups that gave obedience to charismatic leaders.

Even the most virulent antagonists of the cult movements admit that the Jonestown tragedy was an exceptional disaster which had no similar occurrences in modern history. Yet it was constantly depicted as a model of possible repetition. It appears an easy transition, then, from the possible future to the imagined past, and this is where the apostates, the ex-members of the cults, made their most telling propaganda.

What the ex-cultists are now telling about their experiences is almost on a par with those earlier atrocity stories told by ex-priests and ex-nuns against Catholicism. The great majority of ex-members from any church quietly go their way, often with pleasant memories of their association, sometimes in bitterness, but with no determination to destroy their erstwhile comrades. It is the relatively small number of apostates who recount sordid anecdotes, and among these are the victims of deprogramming. "There is no question that the most injurious consequence of deprogramming with respect to the wider social repression of religious movements was the creation of apostates and the dissemination of the anecdotal atrocity stories which they told."[19]

It seems important to note that the horror tales about cultic experiences do not come from former members who simply left the groups quietly like Catholics who stop attending charismatic renewal meetings. But just as there are some ex-charismatics who join fundamentalist religions and preach against the Catholic Church, we find some ex-cultists who become leaders in the anti-cult movement. The most vocal of these opponents are those who were kidnapped and forcibly deprogrammed. It is as though they have to justify themselves for having followed a religion which they now denounce.

These apostates are witnesses at first hand and the only way their falsehoods and exaggerations can be challenged is through the testimony of members who continue happily in the movement, or who left it with no rancor. It is an interesting fact that such testimony does not seem newsworthy. Two magazine cover stories, one in *St. Anthony's Messenger,* the other in *U.S. News and World Report,* printed the revelation of disaffected ex-members, but did not provide balance with the story of a contented member.[20] This appears as sufficient evidence that the new religious movements are judged to be dangerous and destructive. Journalists seem averse to present a balanced story when they deal with cults, even after the lies have been unmasked. A case in point is the movie *A Ticket to Heaven,* which portrayed the story of a Canadian Moonie based on a newspaper series by reporter Josh Freed in 1977. Even though this story was exposed as a fraud by a reputable expert, it continues to gain circulation.[21]

While the motivation of renegades and apostates may be traced to the frightening experience of abduction and deprogramming, it is not clear why others are drawn into a crusade of hate and antagonism against the cults. What inspired the wide circulation of the bogus Knights of Columbus oath when Al Smith ran for President? What was the reason for distributing the fake *Protocols of Zion* during the 1930s? Anti-Catholicism and anti-Semitism were supposed to have died out in the last century. The Mormons and the Quakers, as well as the Catholics and the Jews, were singled out for persecution at earlier times in American history. Religious hostility and hatred were fomented by the Native American Party in the 1830s, the Know Nothing Party in the 1850s, the American Protective Association in the 1890s, and the Ku Klux Klan in this century.

Unfortunately, some of us have not learned the lessons of the past. We do live in peace, more or less, among the conventional churches and denominations. We boast the large pluralist mosaic, but many of us are uncomfortable with the newer religious groups who do not fit neatly into that mosaic pattern. Religious peace is now being disturbed by the bigots and haters. Danger and destruction are coming from the anti-cultists, not from the cultists. Interfering with a member's religious practice, especially to the extent of forcible abduction, is a present danger to freedom of religion, guaranteed to every American.[22] The fact is, however, that the religious youth movements are seen to pose a threat to many Americans, and we must look more deeply into the series of allegations that help to understand this threat.

The Bases of Antagonisms

Why are we suspicious and antagonistic? The religious cults that attract young Americans are peculiar and outlandish precisely because they take God so seriously. In a secular culture of highly materialistic values, the person who commits himself or herself completely to religion has to be viewed with some suspicion, even by the conventional American churchgoer. The fact of religious intensity, serious spirituality, has to be seen as a distinguishing characteristic of the cults. Steven Gelberg, known as Subhananda, of the Denver Krishna Center says: "We're involved in full-time devotion to our religion. Americans are scared of our intensity. To most Americans religion is going to church once a week, then forgetting it. Our religion requires full-time devotion, and that's not the American way."[23]

This other-worldly attitude implies a mockery of precious American values, a conspiracy against capitalism, materialism, consumerism, the free enterprise system. Some commentators note a "tension" between the cult and the larger society. "Cult movements are fully fledged religious organizations which attempt to satisfy all the religious needs of converts." It follows that "the more a cult mobilizes its membership, the greater the opposition it engenders."[24] Cult members find fault with the worldly materialism of American life, and are seen as a source of discord and tension. By their very vocation, of course, the members are opposed to the forces of evil in the world.

From any rational point of view highly spiritual young people ought to be respected and admired, but bigotry is never rational. Good churchgoing parents used to be very disturbed when their teenagers lost interest in religion and stopped going to church. It is difficult to appreciate that the opposite now seems to be happening. Parents are now concerned that a son or daughter has been converted, suddenly got religion and joined a strange and different church. "If they want religion," say the parents, "why do they have to go to some other church?" The objection is even more strenuous when the son or daughter succumbs to the spiritual influence of exotic foreign missionaries.

"The conventional pattern of messianic and missionary activity," says Irving Horowitz, has been from west to east. "The entire history of Western Christendom, indeed the entire history of Christianity under capitalist aegis, has been to colonize the heathen, convert the barbarian. It has always been a movement of white people converting colored people, advanced nations instructing backward nations. And here comes the Reverend Moon and his movement, indisputably Oriental, unquestionably nonwhite, and beyond the pale of Christianity, representing a small state but making his biggest impact on the center of world civilization itself, the United States."[25]

This may not be recognized as a deliberate insult to Christian American parents, and the irony of this reversal seems to have been lost on interpreters of the new religions. This notion has to be "inconceivable in theory and unacceptable in practice, for the conclusion must be that the heathens are western and white and that the truly devout are eastern and colored." Harvey Cox notes a slightly different perspective of this phenomenon, but also the interpretation that these new religions may promote values that are contrary to the American culture of the success syndrome.

"There was very little objection to the Hare Krishna movement when its members were busy proselytizing hippies in Haight-Ashbury and delivering them from hard-drug abuse, presenting an alternative life within the counterculture. It was only when the Hare Krishna movement began presenting an alternative to the culture which endorses graduate school, nuclear family, and career success as the way of life, and when people began joining, that this whole cluster of myths emerged and the Krishna consciousness movement became its target."[26]

Among the myths that justify antagonism to these new religious movements is one that ought to be well known to history-minded Catholics and Jesuits. It is called the "dissimulation myth," known also as the principle of mental reservation among the Jesuits. "This meant that Jesuits could consciously lie, deceive and distort whenever they thought some higher truth was to be served. We still have in the English language the terms 'jesuitical' and 'jesuitism,' which refer to the elaborate rationalization of the means if an end is thought to be worthy."[27]

It is usually the apostate, or defector, from the cult who explains why it had seemed perfectly reasonable to use "heavenly deception," while the members themselves vehemently deny that this is a church "doctrine."[28] This was certainly the case after Maria Monk escaped from the convent in Montreal and disclosed how the priest had explained the essential difference between a religious lie and a wicked lie. "A lie told merely for the injury of another, for our own interest alone, or for no object at all, he painted as a sin worthy of penance. But a lie told for the good of the church or convent was meritorious, and of course the telling of it a duty."[29]

Closely allied to the alleged practice of heavenly deception, or mental reservation, is the charge that the cults win members through a "seductive, manipulative indoctrination process" called programming, or brainwashing. The assumption is, of course, that young people readily convert to Catholicism and other mainstream churches, but they have to be tricked and coerced into membership with the Hare Krishnas, or Unificationists, or Scientologists, or other cultic religions. The concept of religious conversion is as old as the rivalry between peoples of different religious affiliation. "Before the present era of ecumenical goodwill and interfaith understanding, the Jew who became a Christian was obviously coerced to do so. The young Protestant who converted to Catholicism was certainly bewitched by the wiles and deceptions of Rome. The so-called 'fallen-away' Catholic who joined a Protestant Church had come under some evil influence that prevented him from thinking clearly. Ecumenism now absolves the switching of members among the large-scale American religions: the charge of brainwashing is brought only when people are 'victimized' and 'tricked' into joining some new religious cult, especially one with an Oriental flavor."[30]

If the techniques of programming, or mind control, are essential for conversion to the cults, they have not worked very well for the Moonie "brainwashers." The irresistible experience is supposed to be the weekend retreat or workshop, but the fact is that about nine out of ten who attend these retreats do not become Moonies.[31] On the other hand, the notorious deprogrammers Ted Patrick, Joe Alexander and Galen Kelly readily admit that they employ physical restraint and direct coercion, as well as mind control. Nor are they completely successful as seen by the number of their victims who return to the cults.

Another basis for parental complaint against conversion to the cultic religions is that the young people make a total commitment to the new faith. It is not just a matter of going to church more often, reading the Bible every night or saying the rosary every morning. It is a complete vocation. Like the Catholic teenager entering the seminary or novitiate, "the new convert leaves home and family, brothers and sisters, to dedicate himself entirely to the religious calling. Parents sometimes charge that their children have been 'brainwashed.' Similar charges have been made about Catholic religious orders that lured a daughter to the convent or a son to the seminary. God's call must be obeyed even if parents are in opposition."[32] Richard Blake, editor of *America,* remarks that young Moonies embrace a strict, even puritanical lifestyle, even while "the mainstream churches search almost frantically for some way to stop the drift of young people into functional secularism and a culture of do-your-own-thing, casual sex, drugs, and rootlessness."[33]

Young Moonies transfer love and loyalty to their "true parents" in the large spiritual family in which they now live, but they also repudiate the cultural values that parents tried to inculcate, training for professional status, upward mobility in the success-oriented society, proper marriage with a social equal. In other words, the converts to the cult are telling their parents that such worldly ambitions are really not worth striving for, that the parental models and style of life are not worth imitating. This seems particularly irritating when young people switch allegiance to one of the eastern cults like Hare Krishna.

The Christian Response

The rational, humanitarian, democratic, and ecumenical response to these strange religious cults requires that we understand them, that we respect their right to be different, that we attempt to discuss intelligently their religious doctrines and practices. It is an interesting and disconcerting fact that Reverend Jim Jones and his People's Temple were examined from every perspective except that of church religion. In recounting the tragedy of Jonestown no one seemed to notice that this was a duly constituted member of the Churches of Christ and that Jones was a licensed, practicing clergyman of the church.

One model of a *religious* approach to a cult is the document issued by the Commission of Faith and Order of the National Council of Churches in Christ. This was a critique of Moonie theology as interpreted by four Christian theologians who concluded that "the Unification Church is not a Christian church," but who insisted also that "the commission is wholeheartedly committed to the inalienable rights of civil and religious liberties enjoyed in the United States by all religious groups, whether they are the critics or the criticized."

They had studied the scriptures, the "official doctrinal text" of the church, and they said that "this critique of *Divine Principle* does not in any way call into question the freedom of the Unification Church to exist and propagate its beliefs under the protections of the First Amendment."[34]

The Unificationists, of course, insist that they are a Christian religion and carry the official title of the Holy Spirit Association for the Unification of World Christianity. They are not crushed or discouraged by the conclusions of their religious critics. As a matter of fact, they are the only organized religious body I know of that is willing to finance a conference of non-Moonies deliberately established to discuss and criticize their church. Sometimes the critics are quite friendly, as in the book edited by Herbert Richardson, *Ten Theologians Respond to the Unification Church,* but others were sharply critical, as were the Evangelicals who were invited to dialogue with the Moonies at the Barrytown Seminary in the summer of 1978.[35]

Another example of the religious approach is the study made by Stanford professor and theologian Frederick Sontag, who spent ten months in a personal investigation of the Unification Church. As a fair and objective analyst of this new religious movement, he demonstrates a sympathetic understanding of beliefs and practices with which he is not fully in agreement. His synopsis of the fourteen charges that are most often made against Moon and the Moonies is a model of balanced reporting which takes their religious and ecclesial system seriously.[36] His book provides an opportunity for the unprejudiced "outsider" to make rational judgments.

The *ecumenical* approach to the analysis of the cult movements goes a step further by making a positive effort to seek out the truth in any particular cult. Above all, we are told by the Fathers of the Second Vatican Council that we must make "every effort to eliminate words, judgments, and actions which do not respond to the condition of separated brethren with truth and fairness and so make mutual relations between them more difficult." The expectation here, which many antagonists completely ignore, is that good relations, dialogue and interaction are desirable between Catholics and non-

Catholics. The purpose is that "everyone gains a truer knowledge and more just appreciation of the teaching and religious life of both Communions."[37]

Instead of "hammering the heretics," which seems to be the popular reaction of conventional churchgoers, we are enjoined to recognize that which is true in the doctrines of our separated Christian brethren, as well as in the non-Christian religions, Judaism, Hinduism, Buddhism, Islam. Pope John specifically forbade the Council to issue anathemas, condemnations, reprovals or repudiations. This does not mean a readiness to accept theological error, or to embrace ethical mistakes, but it does mean that "the church rejects, as foreign to the mind of Christ, any discrimination against men or harassment of them because of their race, color, condition of life, or religion."[38] In other words, there is an official encouragement for Catholic scholars to associate with the conferences which bring together representatives of different cults.

Logically and morally connected with both the religious and the ecumenical interpretation of the cult phenomenon is the *libertarian* defense of religious liberty. Almost as an early warning to the coercive kidnappers and deprogrammers of our day, the Second Vatican Council reiterated that every human person has a right to religious freedom and explained "this freedom means that all men are to be immune from coercion on the part of individuals or of social groups and of any human power, in such wise that in matters religious no one is to be forced to act in a manner contrary to his own beliefs."[39] This could be applied directly to anti-cult associations, like the Committee on Destructive Cultism (CDC), the Committee Engaged in Freeing Minds (CEFM), the Freedom of Thought Foundation (FTF), the International Foundation for Individual Freedom (IFIF), and other groups who are included in the general category of the "New Vigilantes," by Shupe and Bromley.

Protecting our fellow citizens against kidnapping is even more serious than establishing some kind of antidefamation league to protect the reputation of the cults. The threat of legalized deprogramming is increased by the various proposals to allow temporary conservatorship by court order of cult members. Thomas Robbins discussed this possibility when he insisted that "Even a Moonie has Civil Rights,"[40] and one of the strongest defenders of religious liberty has been the Reverend Dean Kelley, an official of the National Council of Churches. He showed that the attempt to deprogram was not limited to cult members like Children of God, Moonies, or Krishnas, but other cases: a Mormon, a Catholic charismatic, an Episcopalian charismatic, a lesbian, a member of the Socialist Labor Party, and even two young women whose Greek Orthodox parents wanted to get them back into the church.[41]

In the final analysis, it is likely that we fear and distrust that which is strange and unknown to us. To meet personally with young members of some of the cults is a kind of revelation to most of us. They are a bit unusual, of course, if one is accustomed to the materialistic, secular and ambitious American youth who represents the typical middle-class values of our society. When Steve Allen's son wrote to him in 1971 with the news that he had joined a cult, the Church of Armageddon in Seattle, he replied in part as follows: "My feeling in regard to this matter, I suppose, is much like that of those parents whose children decide to enter one of the contemplative orders of the Catholic Church, to become a monk or a nun secluded from the world and to devote their lives to prayer in relative solitude. Here again, selfishly speaking, the parents' hearts ache at the knowledge that they will henceforth be deprived of the sight of those they love. But if they share their children's faith, their sorrow is balanced by a sense of happiness that the children are doing what brings *them* a sense of spiritual satisfaction."[42]

Footnotes

1 The General Secretary of USCC was Bishop Thomas C. Kelley, O.P., now Archbishop of Louisville. The brochure was prepared and published by Boystown Center in Nebraska

2 News article by Paul L. Montgomery, *The New York Times*, Sunday, August 1, 1982

3   Flo Conway and Jim Siegelman, *Snapping: America's Epidemic of Sudden Personality Change*, New York, Lippincott, 1978. See also their article, "Information Disease: Have Cults Created a New Mental Illness?" *Science Digest*, January 1982, pp. 86-92. See the criticism of their data by Brock Kilbourne, "The Conway and Siegelman Claims Against Religious Cults," *Journal for the Scientific Study of Religion*, vol. 22, December 1983, pp. 380-385
4   Harvey Cox, *The Secular City*, New York, Macmillan, 1965, p. 20
5   Peter Berger, *The Heretical Imperative*, Garden City, Doubleday, 1979, p. 184. The third Middletown study by Theodore Caplow, Howard Bahr and Bruce Chadwick, *All Faithful People*, Minneapolis, University of Minnesota Press, 1983, notes "the persistence and renewal of religion in a changing society." p. 38
6   CARA *Report*, vol. 6, June 1982, "Values Study Has International Impact." See also news story, "Traditional Religions Still Vital," *National Catholic Reporter*, June 11, 1982
7   Jeffry K. Hadden and Charles E. Swann, *Prime Time Preachers*, Reading, Addison-Wesley, 1981, p. 55
8   The method is explained in two books by Ira Progoff, *At a Journal Workshop*, 1975, and *The Practice of Process Meditation*, 1980, New York, Dialogue House. See also my commentary, "Retreat Method Seeks Inner Tranquility," *National Catholic Reporter*, September 10, 1982, pp. 10-11
9   Joseph H. Fichter, "The Trend to Spiritual Narcissism," *The Commonweal*, March 17, 1978, pp. 169-173; also *The Cult of the Paraclete*, New York, Sheed and Ward, 1975
10 Dean M. Kelley, *Why Conservative Churches Are Growing: A Study in Sociology of Religion*, New York, Harper and Row, 1972
11 Ernst Troeltsch, *The Social Teaching of the Christian Churches*, New York, Harper, 1960, pp. 993-997
12 Geoffrey Nelson, "The Concept of Cult," *The Sociological Review*, vol. 16, 1968, pp. 351-362
13 A reliable source is Arthur Fauset, *Black Gods of the Metropolis: Negro Religious Cults of the Urban North*, Philadelphia, University of Pennsylvania Press, 1944
14 John Lofland, *Doomsday Cult: A Study of Conversion, Proselytization, and Maintenance of Faith*, Englewood Cliffs, Prentice-Hall, 1966
15 Anson Shupe and David Bromley, *The New Vigilantes, Deprogrammers, Anti-cultists, and the New Religions*, Beverly Hills, Sage, 1980, p. 122
16 Ronald Enroth, *The Lure of the Cults*, Chappaqua, Christian Herald Books, 1979, p. 13. See, however, the excellent rebuttal by James T. Richardson, "People's Temple and Jonestown: A Corrective Comparison and Critique," *Journal for the Scientific Study of Religion*, vol. 19, September 1980, pp. 239-255
17 Cited by Gillian Lindt, "Journeys to Jonestown," *Union Seminary Quarterly Review*, Fall/Winter, 1981-82
18 Jim Siegelman and Flo Conway, "Playboy Interview: Ted Patrick," *Playboy*, March 1979, pp. 53ff
19 See Anson Shupe and David Bromley, "Apostates and Atrocity Stories: Some Parameters in the Dynamics of Deprogramming," pp. 179-215, in Bryan Wilson, ed., *The Social Impact of New Religious Movements*, New York, Rose of Sharon Press, 1981.

20   "Sara: Recovery from a Cult," pp. 30-32, *St. Anthony Messenger,* July 1982; also "The Moonie Life and How One Left It," p. 41, *U.S. News & World Report,* July 5, 1982

21   Bart Testa, "Making Crime Seem Natural: The Press and Deprogramming," pp. 41-81, in M. Darrol Bryant and Herbert Richardson, eds., *A Time for Consideration,* New York, Mellen Press, 1978; also the movie reviews by Donald E. Messer, "Rescuing the Cult Member," *The Christian Century,* February 24, 1982, which reviews *Ticket to Heaven,* a film based on Josh Freed, *Moonwebs*

22   See my article, "Hammering the Heretics: Religions vs. Cults," *The Witness,* January 1983, pp. 4-6, which is the basis for much of the present chapter

23   Quoted by Steve Allen, *Beloved Son,* pp. 200-201. Gelberg, however, is suspicious of other cults and sects, in particular the Moonies, whom he calls "quite coercive and deceptive."

24   See Rodney Stark and William Brainbridge, "Concepts for a Theory of Religious Movements," pp. 3-25, in Joseph H. Fichter, ed., *Alternatives to American Mainline Churches,* New York, Rose of Sharon Press, 1982

25   Irving Louis Horowitz, ed., *Science, Sin and Scholarship,* Cambridge, MIT Press, 1978, p. xv

26   Harvey Cox, "Myths Sanctioning Persecution," pp. 3-19, in Bryant and Richardson, *op. cit.*

27   *Ibid.,* p. 9

28   See discussion, pp. 84-99, in Richard Quebedeaux and Rodney Sawatsky, eds., *Evangelical-Unification Dialogue,* New York, Rose of Sharon Press, 1979

29   *Awful Disclosures of Maria Monk,* New York, 1936, Arno Press reprint, 1977, p. 72

30   Joseph H. Fichter, "Youth in Search of the Sacred," pp. 21-41, Bryan Wilson, ed., *The Social Impact of New Religious Movements,* New York, Rose of Sharon Press, 1981

31   *Ibid.,* pp. 59-96, Eileen Barker, "Who'd Be a Moonie? A Comparative Study of Those Who Join the Unification Church in Britain." See also J. Stillson Judah, "New Religions and Religious Liberty," pp. 201-208, in Jacob Needleman and George Baker, eds., *Understanding the New Religions,* New York, Seabury, 1978

32   Joseph H. Fichter, "Marriage, Family and Sun Myung Moon," *America,* October 27, 1979, pp. 226-228

33   Richard A. Blake, "The Attraction of the Moonies," *America,* February 2, 1980, pp. 83-85

34   This document is published, pp. 102-118, in Irving Louis Horowitz, ed., *Science, Sin and Scholarship,* Cambridge, MIT Press, 1978

35   See Richard Quebedeaux and Rodney Sawatsky, ed., *Evangelical-Unification Dialogue,* New York, Rose of Sharon Press, 1979, as contrasted with Herbert Richardson, ed., *Ten Theologians Respond to the Unification Church,* New York, Rose of Sharon Press, 1981

36   Frederick Sontag, *Sun Myung Moon and the Unification Church,* Nashville, Abingdon, 1977, pp. 176-200, for "The Charges That Inflame Us"

37   *Unitatis Redintegratio,* Decree on Ecumenism, article 4

38   *Nostra Aetate,* Declaration on the Relationship of the Church to Non-Christian Religions, article 5

39   *Dignitatis Humanae,* Declaration on Religious Freedom, article 2

40 Thomas Robbins, "Deprogramming the Brainwashed: Even a Moonie Has Civil Rights," *The Nation,* February 26, 1977, pp. 238-242

41 Dean M. Kelley, "Deprogramming and Religious Liberty," *The Civil Liberties Review,* July/August 1977, pp. 23-33. See also Jean Caffey Lyles' story about Dean Kelley in "The Religious Rights of the Unlovely," *The Christian Century,* June 2, 1982, pp. 652-653. See also Donald L. Drakeman, "Cult Members: Converts or Criminals?" *The Christian Century,* February 15, 1984, pp. 163-165

42 Steve Allen, *Beloved Son, A Story of the Jesus Cults,* New York, Bobbs-Merrill, 1982, pp. 9-10. The author then describes not only the Love Family to which his son belonged, but also the Brotherhood of the Source, the Children of God, the Unification Church, the Brotherhood of the Sun, Synanon, and Hare Krishna

II The Moonie as Ex-Catholic

The Unification Church appears to hold a special attraction for young Catholics who not only swell the ranks of the membership but also rise to some of the higher positions in the movement. One of the reasons I was drawn to further study of the Unification Church was the interviews I had with these Catholics who had converted to the church. In fewer numbers I talked also with young Catholics who had joined other so-called "cults" and I looked for a pattern of experiences within the Catholic Church that would explain their resignation from the church. An unexpected finding in this regard is that they had not been dissatisfied with Catholicism.

The former Catholics who joined the Moonies are for the most part friendly to the Catholic Church. They had no complaints against the clergy in their parish, or against the religious Sisters who taught them in the parochial school. They did not find fault with the doctrines of the church, or with the usual "obstacles" that some Protestants allege against Catholicism: papal infallability, the virgin birth, devotion to Mary, the practice of confession, or the prohibition against birth control. They were not complaining about the "rules" of the church, like obligatory mass attendance. Indeed, they were quite ready to say that there is "nothing wrong" in Catholicism that would motivate them to abandon their faith.

In several instances I was told, "I'm a better Catholic now than I was before." They felt that they really did not "leave" the church but had learned to develop more fully the virtues and practices of Catholicism. They were attracted to practices of group prayer and singing. They appreciated the religious significance of periodic fasting. They went on spiritual retreats for three days or a week, and became so thoroughly knowledgeable of the *Divine Principle* that they could give lectures on it. The spirituality they learned as Catholics is now intensified and they claim they have a greater personal feeling for Jesus, a greater devotion to the Father, and have built on the religious foundations they had accepted as Catholics. One can argue whether they really were genuine Catholics, whether they had really understood the teachings of the Catholic faith.

Did they have a valid Catholic background? The most pious Moonies seem to come from pious Catholic families. In many instances both parents were regularly practicing Catholics; and in some families—as among Catholics generally—the mother was more devout than the father. The children attended mass, sang in the choir, belonged to the sodality or the youth club and were generally good parishioners. Most of the converts to the Unification Church had had formal Catholic schooling, many through high school, and some through Catholic college. Some of the emerging leaders had all their education, including college or university, under Catholic auspices, and had passed all the required courses in theology or religious studies.

The claim that they are now "more Catholic" than they were implies that the Moonie beliefs and practices they now embrace are an improvement—not a repudiation—of Catholicism. They are, of course, well aware of the differences, but these are seen as an advance toward God, the result of revelation and new insight into religion. One of the "improvements" they most appreciate is less theological than sociological. This is their experience of love and community at a personal level which they see as a reflection of the principle of a universal brotherhood. Their love of God must embrace all people regardless of race, nationality or religion. When I reminded them that the Mystical Body of Christ is this same doctrine of the Roman Catholic Church, they responded "Yes, but these people practice it."

The Unification God

The definition of God in dualistic terms must seem strange to any educated Catholic, especially when we are told that God's essential character is masculine and essential form is feminine. Unification theology "starts with the fact of polarity as the main clue for understanding the essential nature of God. Hence, it is not primarily interested in defending the trinitarian doctrine of the fourth-century creeds."[1] Although Christians have traditionally prayed to God, the Father, their theologians have clearly taught that God is sexless, neither male nor female. Everything we know about God must be expressed in analogies because God's essential nature lies beyond our comprehension.

The ancient Christian trinitarian creed is regularly professed by mainline Christian churches and is recited by Catholics during the Sunday mass at their parish church. When Catholics bless themselves, the sign of the cross is made "in the name of the Father and of the Son and of the Holy Spirit." While the blessed Trinity remains a divine mystery to both theologians and laity, it is well stated as one God in three persons. The Holy Spirit is worshipped and glorified together with the Father and the Son. There is no room in Unificationist theology for the divine trinity because neither Christ nor the Holy Spirit is acknowledged as divine.

The center of attention and of worship among the Moonies is God, the Father and Creator of all things, who is recognized and loved in a very personal way. He is both the source of love and the object of love; and not the aloof, omnipotent, omniscient and immutable divine being of the medieval philosophers. The Moonie believes that God's heart is torn by the sins of his children; God suffers because of the evils in the world. This is not merely a figure of speech. The suffering of God is real. One is reminded of the Catholic devotion to the Sacred Heart of Jesus, and especially of the realistic sermons of Good Friday when the Sacred Heart was depicted as the terrible target and subject of all human evils. This Catholic devotion has diminished in popularity but the ex-Catholics among the Moonies see the similarity with the broken heart of God.

God is intimately and personally present to the Moonie, and is apparently subject to change, to joy and to sorrow, in a way that born-again Christians sometimes describe their relationship with Jesus. The flexible God of process theology is more acceptable to

Moonies than to Catholics. God can be reached in prayer; he can be affected by the practices of "indemnity" on the part of his sinful creatures. Many Moonies are "convinced that they now understand 'God's heart,' the principle of his action, and the plan according to which he would now have them act and serve him."[2]

Incomplete Redeemer

One of the most startling Moonie doctrines is the refusal to accept Jesus as the redeemer. The Catholic teaching is clear: that the redemption of sinful humanity was accomplished by the life, death and resurrection of Jesus. This is the message of salvation delivered from all Christian pulpits, bishops in great cathedrals, famous televangelists and fundamentalist preachers. God's redemptive and efficacious forgiveness of sins finds its definitive culmination in Jesus Christ. There is no other redeemer. The central fact of Christianity is that Jesus is Lord. The core of the Christian message is that Jesus is God and Savior, that he was sent by the Father to die for the sins of mankind.

The words of *Divine Principle* are unmistakably the opposite: the purpose of Jesus' coming as messiah was to restore the kingdom of heaven on earth, and to fulfill the providence of restoration. "The Christ would govern the covenanted people of God with justice and righteousness as prophesied in Isaiah."[3] This could not be accomplished if he died. "Jesus' crucifixion was the result of the ignorance and disbelief of the Jewish people and was not God's predestination to fulfill the whole purpose of Jesus' coming as the messiah."[4] The people did not believe in him; they persecuted and crucified him, and his mission was a failure.

The revelation of the *Divine Principle* maintains, however, that the mission of Jesus was not entirely in vain. Redemption by the cross provides only "spiritual salvation" but not physical salvation. "Jesus could not accomplish the purpose of the providence of physical salvation because his body was invaded by Satan. However, he could establish the basis for spiritual salvation by forming a triumphant foundation for resurrection through the redemption by the blood of the cross."[5] With all this, Christ is still no more than a human. The Moonies do not accept the divinity of Christ; after all, they do not invite Jesus into the Blessed Trinity, which is also repudiated by the Unificationists. As Foster remarks, "*Divine Principle* stops short of the full traditional affirmation of Christic divinity as that was established at Nicaea, Constantinople and Chalcedon. A pivotal formulation of its view is that while Jesus 'may well be called God,' because he exemplified individual human perfection, 'he can by no means be God himself.' "[6]

The Incarnation is the mystery of the hypostatic union, the fact evident in scripture that Jesus Christ is true God and true man. When Jesus declared himself to be the messiah, "son of the blessed God,"[7] the High Priest condemned him for blasphemy. Christology must obviously be studied in close connection with soteriology, which deals with his redemptive work, and this in turn must be closely connected with trinitarian theology. The complex systematic theology of Christianity falls apart when some of its key segments are removed. If Jesus himself does not have the divine nature as the second person of the blessed Trinity, the traditional Christian doctrine of his divine messiahship must be abandoned.

This is not the place to argue about the truth of this or that theological doctrine, but simply to indicate in general terms that the Unification teaching about Jesus the Messiah is clearly at odds with the orthodox doctrines accepted through the centuries in the mainstream of Western Christianity.[8] The ex-Catholics among the young Moonies who explain their new beliefs about Jesus and his role as the failed messiah seem undisturbed by their repudiation of Christian beliefs. Their response to this matter is the general explanation of their position in all questions of this kind: "I am still a Christian but I don't believe it the same way as the Catholics do." They are now future-oriented, as is customary among millenarians, and await further revelation through the messiah, Reverend Moon, who is God's human messenger for the restoration of humanity.

Original Sin

The story of the Fall of Man, as revised by Reverend Moon, is the first revelation that most young Moonies learn and which they accept as a dramatic explanation of human sinfulness. The description as taught in the second chapter of *Divine Principle* claims to be both new and unique because "until the present era, not a single man has known the root of sin."[9] It was the sin of lust between an angel and a woman, a most extraordinary miscegenation, that is now said to be the beginning of evil among God's human creatures. This story is so fanciful, and so titillating, that it immediately captures the attention and imagination of Moonie neophytes. It is also in direct contrast to traditional mainstream Christian theology.

Orthodox Christian theology teaches that the first man was created in sanctifying grace, or in the state of "original justice." As the *Divine Principle* suggests, "This man is not in need of redemption or of a savior, nor does he need the life of prayer and faith required by fallen men, because he is without original sin."[10] In Catholic theology the fall of man signifies chiefly the free decision of Adam to turn away from God, in other words, Adam's own personal sin of pride and disobedience. It had nothing to do with illicit intercourse or with the eating of forbidden fruit, and it must be distinguished from "original sin" of Adam's descendants, which can be termed sin only in an analogous sense.

The generally accepted Christian tradition is that Satan and the other devils were naturally good when God created them, but they became evil of their own accord. This means that the good angel Lucifer became the fallen angel, Satan, well before the creation of Adam and Eve and their subsequent transgression in the Garden of Eden. The *Divine Principle* has it that the angel became Satan as a result of—and in punishment for—his immoral act of lust with Eve, the sin of fornication, and had not been in earlier prideful rebellion against the Creator. What happened subsequent to this illicit sexual intercourse is that Satan and his evil spirits have held sovereignty over the world. In Unification morality emphasis is placed on the teaching that adultery is not only the most horrendous sin among human beings but that it is the very root of all sinfulness.[11] It is worse than any other kind of moral transgression and it must be suppressed before there can be any hope of restoration and human salvation.

With this emphasis on the universality of sinful sexuality, one may readily understand why the Moonies focus on marriage and family as the bastion of morality and as the channel of salvation. The only way that original sin can be washed from the individual Moonie is through Blessed marriage. This is also the way in which the inherited lineage of original sin can be interrupted. The children of blessed couples are conceived and born without original sin, and they are blessed children. "As Unification couples, we feel that it is God's blessing for us to have families, and we believe that our position as Blessed couples is different before God. We are part of a new, heavenly lineage—free from the hold (but not from the influence) of evil."[12]

A solemn addendum was made by Young Oon Kim that "the worst result of the Fall is its effect upon God. His purpose of creation became frustrated. As a consequence of the Fall, God was virtually deprived of his sovereignty over creation. He lost his hold over the human heart. If God is the God of heart, his heart must have been broken by the seduction of Adam and Eve. For untold centuries God has suffered. How long his disappointment, dismay, bitterness, and grief have accumulated."[13]

The Missing Virgin Mary

Since Christ does not hold the central place in the Unification interpretation of salvation history, one seeks in vain for the so-called "infancy narratives" that characterize the gospels according to Matthew and Luke. There is no story of the star or of the angels singing. There is no Christmas creche, watched over by Mary and Joseph, and visited by the shepherds and the wise men. According to Reverend Moon, Jesus was the offspring of two people of pure lineage, but not the son of a virgin mother who conceived by the power of the Holy Spirit. The celebration of Christmas is "low key" among the

Moonies. The Catholic child who learned from early years to pray the "Hail Mary" finds this prayer meaningless upon accepting the Unification faith. One does not see a statue, or a picture, of the Blessed Virgin in the home or the workplace of a Unificationist, nor is there the traditional praying of the rosary or of a novena to Our Lady in the life of the ex-Catholic Moonie.

In modern Catholic theology Mary has come to be known as the co-redemptrix, the second Eve, the Mother of God, who was conceived and born free of original sin,[14] and who led a virtuous life on earth. Theologians and spiritual writers have given her the title of "mediatrix" to convey the notion that all supernatural grace comes to us through her intercession with God because of her unique position in salvation history. To use Unification terminology, Mary was from the beginning endowed with the divine "first blessing" which signifies the perfection of her individuality, and her personal spiritual relationship with God. She possesses to a supreme degree the supernatural sinless state in which the children of Blessed couples are said to be born. Mary is the "paragon of human redemption, the most perfectly redeemed, and therefore the archtype of all the redeemed."[15]

Devout Unificationists see themselves as the spiritual children of their "true parents," Sun Myung and Hak Ja Moon. I have not heard any of them refer to her as their "Blessed Mother," which is a term always used by devout Catholics in reference to Mary, the Mother of God. It is questionable whether the former Catholic who is now a Moonie replaces personal devotion to the Virgin Mary with that of the new and spiritual mother, Mrs. Moon. The Moonie concept of the family as a generational channel of redemption is hardly comparable with the traditional devotion to the "Holy Family" of Jesus, Mary and Joseph.

Devotion to Mary is so integral to the personal life of Catholics that it appears to be synonymous with Catholic culture of every ethnic background. She is venerated as the national patroness in many parts of the Christian world and her well-known shrines have become the object of pilgrimage and the locus of miracles. In France the shrine of Our Lady of Lourdes attracts international gatherings, as does Our Lady of Fatima in Portugal and Our Lady of Guadalupe in Mexico. The person who has been raised in the midst of these spiritual practices is not likely to lose memories of them when shifting to another religion. One wonders what substitutes can be provided to allow the same level of spiritual enthusiasm.

The Lack of Sacraments

It must seem strange for most Christians to live in a church that does not baptize its new members, especially the infants. The Moonie dedication ceremony on the eighth day of the child's life is a substitute ritual, but no one calls it baptism.[16] There has to be, in the memory of the Moonie ex-Catholic, a picture of the festivities surrounding the formal christening of an infant sibling in the parish church. Later, the youngster's reception of "First Holy Communion" is an occasion for parochial and familial celebration. In most families it has been the custom to have a photograph taken and preserved in the family album of cherished memories. The sacrament of confirmation is also an important public ceremony when the young Catholic for the first time has personal contact with the bishop of the diocese and is "strengthened" in the Faith.

From earliest childhood the practicing Catholic is living a sacramental life and his religious identity is recognized by the fact that he "goes to the sacraments." This means regular attendance at mass and frequent reception of the eucharist in holy communion. To receive the eucharist implies that a person is in the "state of grace," that is, not having committed any serious sin, or having "gone to confession" for the remission of such sin. The sacrament of penance was traditionally bound up intimately with communion, but in recent years the practice of auricular confession has for some given way to the collective forgiveness of sins.

Although a small number of ex-Catholic Moonies reveal that they occasionally attend mass and receive communion, the better instructed among them realize that this practice—and its theological meanings—is of no significance in the Unification Church. Since they do not believe in the incarnation—that Jesus is true man and true God—they are hardly expected to believe in the "real presence" of Jesus in the blessed sacrament. The reality of the eucharist is founded on the last supper, as described in the gospels of Luke and Mark, where Jesus gave himself to the apostles under the appearance of bread and wine. Transubstantiation is as much a mystery as the incarnation. We speak also of the "sacrifice" of the mass as the sacred offering of the victim Jesus to God, the Father.

The concept of sacrament as "an outward sign of inward grace" is probably widely misunderstood as a kind of magic by ill-informed persons. In Catholic theology, "the sacraments contain and communicate (as instrumental causes) the grace which they signify."[17] The *Divine Principle* does not use the language of sacrament, nor does the Unification Church itself, with the exception of the "sacramental aspect" of the holy wine ceremony. The exchange of wine between the couple is said to be "more than symbolic. It represents or communicates something from Reverend Moon's spirituality to the couple."[18] This is the only "central ritual" celebrated by the Moonies. It is the actual marriage ceremony and must not be confused with the widely publicized "mass weddings" that take place later. The ex-Catholic Moonie who has this experience knows that it is very different from the solemn nuptial mass celebrated in the parish church.

There is no sacrament of holy orders, or any ordination ceremony in the Unification Church, although about twenty of the senior members bear the honorary title of Reverend. In the Catholic Church there is a sense in which the lay members share in the "common priesthood of the faithful," although they differ from the "ministerial priest."[19] Relatively few lay Catholics have the opportunity to witness the sacramental ordination of a young man to the priesthood, but most Catholics have been present at the parochial solemn first mass of a newly ordained priest. It is, of course, mainly through the ministry of the parish clergy that Catholics receive the sacraments, an experience the Moonie can no longer validly enjoy.

The Millenarian Mystery

Christian theologians generally describe the *parousia,* the saving presence of Christ, as the consummation of history in God, who will be directly revealed in his glory. Fundamentalist preachers are sure that we are approaching the "end time" and warn their audiences that they must prepare to meet the Lord of the Second Advent. Catholics tend to be much less excited about this prospect, and have been long accustomed to the words "Thy Kingdom Come" in the Lord's Prayer and to those passages of the holy mass that anticipate the return of Christ in glory. An exception to this calm attitude among Catholics is in the renewal movement promoted by Charismatic Pentecostals.[20]

The Catholic who becomes a member of the Unification Church is introduced to an almost apocalyptic cultural mood. Theological speculation gives way to the revealed truth of *Divine Principle.* A whole chapter is devoted to the "Consummation of Human History," and another to the "Advent of the Messiah." Two central teachings were revealed to Reverend Moon concerning eschatology, which had previously been hidden from mankind. The first is that upon the coming of the Lord "as the true parent of mankind, all men will come to live harmoniously in the garden as one family."[21] The restoration of all things in God is not to be feared as a time of horror and suffering, but as a time of great joy. This first revelation is likely to be acceptable to any Christian concerned about the future.

The second important revelation describes in great detail when, how, and where Christ will come again. Jesus had said that no one knew the day and the hour of the second advent, "therefore, up to the present time, it has been thought reckless even to try to know when, where and how the Lord would come." The prophets know that he does not come "in the clouds," but is born of flesh in the chosen nation of Korea. One does not need great imagination to read the name of Reverend Moon into the following passage: modern Christians "will surely criticize the words and conduct of the Lord of the Second Advent, according to the limits of what the New Testament words literally state. So, it is only too clear that they can be expected to persecute him and brand him a heretic."[22]

The identity of the Lord of the Second Advent is not specified, but he is believed to have been born in Korea between 1917 and 1930. The obvious question to ask the Unificationist is whether Reverend Moon fits this description and must be considered the messiah. The critics of the church say that he makes this claim but the Moonies themselves assure us that he has never called himself the messiah. It would indeed be a giant step of conversion for an ex-Catholic to replace the Savior Jesus with the Savior Moon. Nevertheless, one senses an enormous reverence among the members for their spiritual Father. In their eyes he is something more than the charismatic leader of an exotic cult. He is a special messenger sent by God, and with instructions from God, to bring the human race into the messianic age.

Ecumenical Relations

Most of the American Catholics who are now members of the Unification Church are probably too young to remember the time when the church forbade *participatio in divinis* of other churches. Associating with heretics was obviously a danger to the faith of the individual who not only had the obligation to preserve a purity of belief but also to prevent scandal. It was clear that lending support to an erroneous church helped to perpetuate the doctrinal error of that group. If there was to be Christian unity it had to be through the "homecoming" of the Protestant dissidents, as well as of all non-Christians. From the perspective of the Catholic Church, those who joined the Unification movement went in the opposite direction, "away from home."

Everyone knows that the ecumenical movement promoted by the Second Vatican Council was "started and organized for the fostering of unity among Christians." This did not mean a repudiation of any Catholic doctrine but it is now an admission that many sacred actions among the separated brethren "can truly engender a life of grace, and can be rightly described as capable of providing access to the community of salvation."[23] In other words, not everything that is done in a Protestant church is a heretical action, and a Catholic is allowed to be present as an observer at such worship service and may also at times "come together for common prayer." The Council document is ecumenical toward all religions without exception, but in the United States a peculiar interpretation of this document embraces all mainline religions while it excludes the newer and "destructive" religions like the Unification Church.

The Holy Spirit Association for the Unification of World Christianity is built on a foundation different from that of Catholicism. The *Divine Principle* reveals "the historical fact that all religions, which in fact have an identical purpose, are being absorbed gradually into the cultural sphere of Christianity. Therefore, Christianity is not a religion for Christians alone, but has the mission of accomplishing the ultimate purpose of all the religions that have appeared in the past."[24] Presumably, the "identical purpose" of all religions is to cooperate successfully in divine providence, but the history of religions demonstrates an almost infinite variety in the way that human beings work out that purpose.

The fact that the Moonies of my acquaintance are devout and dedicated members of the Unification Church frees them from the charge of religious "indifferentism" which supposedly afflicts ecumenists who are tolerant of other religions. Ex-Catholic Moonies may well be tolerant of Catholicism and every other church, but their minds and hearts are fixed on the Unificationist experience. I have talked seriously with them about all of the items discussed in this chapter. They know that I am intellectually and theologically at odds with the Moonie system of religious belief and practice. In my contacts with them I have carefully followed the steps recommended by the fathers of the Second Vatican Council: to learn the truth about them, to cooperate in projects for the common good, to share common prayer, and to deal with them in love and justice. In this sense, the chapter ends on the same note with which it began.

Footnotes

1 Young Oon Kim, *Unification Theology,* New York, Holy Spirit Association, p. 53. See *Divine Principle,* p. 25

2 Frederick Sontag, "The God of Principle: A Critical Evaluation," pp. 107-139, in Herbert Richardson, ed., *Ten Theologians Respond to the Unification Church,* New York, Rose of Sharon Press, 1981

3 Young Oon Kim, *Unification Theology and Christian Thought,* New York, Golden Gate Press, 1976, p. 101

4 *Divine Principle,* p. 145

5 *Divine Principle,* p. 148

6 Durwood Foster, "Unification and Traditional Christology," pp. 179-199, in Herbert Richardson, ed., *Ten Theologians Respond to the Unification Church,* New York, Rose of Sharon Press, 1981

7 Mark 14/61-62

8 Raymond E. Brown, *Jesus God and Man,* Milwaukee, Bruce, 1967, "Jesus as the Messiah," pp. 79-86

9 *Divine Principle,* chapter 2, "Fall of Man," pp. 63-97

10 *Ibid.,* p. 141

11 *Divine Principle,* "The Root of Sin," pp. 75-76

12 See Hugh and Nora Spurgin, "Engagement, Marriage and Children," pp. 1-49, in Richard Quebedeaux, ed., *Lifestyle,* New York, Rose of Sharon Press, 1982

13 Young Oon Kim, *Unification Theology,* New York, Holy Spirit Association, 1980, p. 124

14 This is the doctrine of the Immaculate Conception of Mary, which is often confused with Christ's virgin birth of Mary

15 See Vatican II document on the church, *Lumen Gentium,* articles 52-69, "The Role of the Blessed Virgin Mary"

16 "This is similar in attitude to a baptism or christening ceremony in other churches." Hugh and Nora Spurgin, "Engagement, Marriage and Children," pp. 1-49, in Richard Quebedeaux, ed., *Lifestyle,* New York, Rose of Sharon Press, 1982

17 Karl Rahner and Herbert Vorgrimler, *Theological Dictionary,* New York, Herder and Herder, 1965, p. 417

18 M. Darrol Bryant and Susan Hodges, eds., *Exploring Unification Theology,* New York, Rose of Sharon Press, 1978, p. 19

19 Vatican II, *Lumen Gentium,* chapter 2, "The People of God"

20 This phenomenon is discussed in my book, *The Catholic Cult of the Paraclete,* New York, Sheed and Ward, 1975

21 *Divine Principle,* chapters 3 and 4, pp. 99-164

22 *Divine Principle,* Part II, chapter 6, pp. 497-536. See also Neil Albert Salonen, "Second Coming Lecture," pp. 246-258, in Darrol Bryant, ed., *Proceedings* of Virgin Islands' Seminar, New York, Rose of Sharon Press, 1980

23 Vatican II, *Unitatis Redentegratio,* articles 3 and 4

24 *Divine Principle,* p. 189

III Youth in Search of the Sacred

The continued existence of the "new" religions in America is a puzzle, if not a challenge, to sociologists who are confident that religion will disappear from Western industrial society before the year 2000.[1] In discussing the most vigorous of these youth religions, C. Daniel Batson remarked that "in spite of the immense importance of religion in the lives of millions of people, psychologists have tended to treat religion as a vestige of pre-scientific civilization soon to disappear and therefore not worthy of consideration."[2] Since religious systems lack cognitive and empirical bases, the fathers of sociology "saw sociology as itself an alternative to theological knowledge."[3] Religion in its ideas, practices and institutions was an anachronism in the development of modern society.

In the first American study of the Moonies, John Lofland wrote that sociologists "pride themselves on their positivistic common sense" and have great difficulty in attempting to explain how cult members maintain religious faith.[4] Social scientists, whether they study religion or any other institution, think of themselves as very rational people who deal only with empirical evidence. Nevertheless, research evidence is accumulating that the conversion to religion and the maintenance of a supernatural faith are rational decisions made by normal people in search of meaning for their lives. Joining a new religion is now most often seen as a "normal process" among those who are looking for something more than, and different from, contemporary materialistic lifestyles.[5]

The focus of this chapter is on young people who say they have encountered God and who believe that that encounter is of central importance to themselves and to society. Instead of trying to rationalize or psychologize the religious experience of young Moonies, I want to take them seriously when they say with their theologian, Young Oon Kim, that "any religious search is man's attempt to restore the original relationship of love with God."[6] In other words, these young people are asserting that religion is precisely what it is defined to be: a probing relationship in search of truth, transcendence, and the sacred. To commune with the Infinite, to be in the presence of God—here we are talking about the essence of religion.

The Crisis of Secularity

It has been part of the positivist conventional wisdom that religion is in crisis and that young people in particular are in rebellion against God. This wisdom is now being questioned, and the forecasts are spoken in a weaker voice. There is research evidence now that "religion is not permanently vulnerable to secularization," and that religious cults are flourishing even while some of the conventional churches are losing influence.[7] The search for transcendence and spirituality is apparent now, perhaps unexpectedly, among young Americans. Wuthnow observes that "virtually all accounts of contemporary religious movements have described them as youth phenomena."[8]

In broadest terms we may say that secularity is a negation of the spiritual and an affirmation of the material. Most often it is seen as a replacement for religion, even an opponent of religion. In a book that was out of date even before it was published in English, Acquaviva talked about the "Eclipse of the Sacred." Like so many of the positivists he was sure that we are witnessing the end of the sacred. He wrote that "from the religious point of view, humanity has entered a long night that will become darker and darker with the passing of the generations, and on which no end can yet be seen." He conceded that perhaps some people may feel a need for religious faith and practice, but humanity is completely enmeshed in "uncertainty, doubt, and existential insecurity."[9]

Taking their usual broad overview of culture and society, social scientists apply Toennies' thesis to a kind of cosmic drift from small, simple, moral, and God-fearing communities to large, complex, individualistic, and sensate societies. The neat, all-embracing formula for this drift combines three simultaneous long-term trends: industrialization, urbanization, and secularization. The quick hypothesis accepted by sociology students is that people who live in cities, in a technological culture, logically lose interest in religion. The acceptance of cultural determinism suggests an almost inevitable and irreversible trend in the succession of Sorokin's cultural stages from idealistic to ideational and to sensate.

Distinctions abound between spiritual and material, natural and supernatural, reason and religion, and there is a recognizable shift from one to the other. Durkheim insisted that every society makes a distinction between that which is profane and that which is sacred. If this is said in measurable terms these phenomena are proportionately different according to the type of religion existing in the society. The sacred is more pronounced in an immanentist religion as among most primitive people and in the religions of Hinduism, Buddhism, and Taoism. The profane is likely to be more emphasized in a transcendental religion, as in Judaism, Islam, and Christianity.

Secularization, then, is a process, a shift, from the sacred and the religious to the profane and the material. A double transformation of thinking occurs in this process: One is a desacralization of attitudes toward persons and things, the other a rationalization of thought which is logical, scientific, objective, and free of emotion. What this means is that the religious world-view, whether immanent or transcendental, is no longer the basic frame of reference. This is the triumph of the secular which has been taken as an article of faith, a practically unshakable dogma of sociological theory.

One can understand why secularism is so attractive to the typical American sociologists, why it fits in so neatly with contemporary idealogical baggage. Secularism is rooted in humanitarianism and democracy. It tends to reflect the rational and scientific forces that are said to be responsible for the enormous progress achieved in the Western world. This philosophical ideal is often called secular humanism, and it is synonymous with morality independent of any value that "transcends the natural, historical and social order of man."[10] It is interesting to note Tillich's remark that the great problem facing Christianity is not the opposition of non-Christian religions but the pervasive strength of secular humanism.[11]

An argument can be made, however, that at least among sociologists the transcendentalism of religion has been replaced by the immanentism of secularism. To the extent that this has occurred in the American population therein lies the crisis of secularism. A peculiarly appropriate label for this phenomenon is "utopian materialism." It has to be called *materialism* because "it reduces man to his most instinctive and spontaneous aspirations, apart from any ethical experience." It has to be called *utopian* because out of these aspirations there should emerge "a degree of consciousness and human fulfillment that can come only from man's ethical development."[12]

This concept of utopian materialism is probably known by another name to students of economic theory who hold the notion that satisfaction of private interest eventually redounds to the benefit of the total society. This is not the same as the celebration of the "me decade," of a narcissism that is automatically and logically anti-social. The paradox and the concept of utopian materialism are that the fever to consume, the gratification of desires, and the satisfaction of possessive instincts are thought to be for the commonweal. Out of these will emerge "the nobler attributes of mankind—liberty, peace, love, fullness, justice—and thus bring about a genuine utopia of happiness."[13]

Secular Enslavement

Utopian materialism is a trap; humanistic secularism leads to its own brand of conformism. This is not how Harvey Cox interpreted the ideology of secularism in his popular celebration of the Secular City. He saw it as "a new closed world-view which functions very much like a new religion." Although he conceded that it can become a menace to openness and freedom, he said that the *process* of secularization is "almost certainly irreversible, in which society and culture are delivered from the tutelage to religious control and closed metaphysical world-views. We have argued that it is basically a liberating development."[14] I want to argue the exact opposite: that large numbers of people have been programmed into a routine of consumerism, materialism, secularism.

Desacralization and rationalization were meant to liberate us from fantasy, emotionalism and sentimentality, but much of the contemporary literature of protest complains that we have been therewith enslaved.[15] Rationality has been rightly credited with enormous progress in Western economies, education and government, but at the price of human freedom. The consequence is that human beings are everywhere regulated and controlled, and confined to tasks and goals that have no deep meaning or value for them. The fact that the sociocultural system has been "rationalized," that is, planned in a logical and technical fashion, does not mean that the people who are routinized into the system are acting and thinking in a logical or rational manner.

It may appear over-dramatic, even sensational, to talk in terms of cultural enslavement, imprisonment, dehumanization, but there is a point at which normal behavioral conformity becomes a kind of abnormal behavioral lockstep. Any introductory textbook in sociology points out that customs and mores have to be institutionalized for the maintenance of an orderly social life. Human beings are socialized, not only as children learning the ways of the culture but all through adulthood by conformity and adaptation to the requirements of the society. Human behavior is modified and institutionalized as an alternative to chaotic social relations and eccentric personal conduct.[16]

This universal fact of socialization must not be interpreted at any simplistic level of psychological compulsion or cultural determinism. Quite aside from religious affiliation, the fact is that our behavior is patterned to the expectations of the various social groups to which we belong: we are indeed programmed to think and act in ways that are acceptable and approved in the larger society. Ruth Benedict said this clearly, but she pointed out that we are the "creatures of culture," while at the same time recognizing that we are also the "creators of our culture."

The impress of our culture is strong upon us, so that we feel odd in acting otherwise. The process of patterning and programming is obviously selective by one's experiences in social relations, which "allow entry of only certain aspects of reality. This is what is meant by one's consciousness: the categories by which one perceives the world." Richard DeMaria notes that the secularized person does not get an entry on religion. "An excessively individualistic ego-centered consciousness, one which has been shaped largely in terms of individual survival in a hostile world, cuts one off from that special perception which is known by many names, but which seems common to so many reports of religious experience."[17]

It appears that there are always some people who reflect on the tyranny of the sensate culture, question it, investigate it, and then raise their awareness of alternatives. We hear constantly of the need for consciousness raising, to become aware that there are alternatives to the system in which we have been socialized. Perhaps it is safe to say that people sense that "something is missing" that could make for a more satisfactory life. This seems to be what the blacks are seeking when they complain that there is no "soul" in contemporary Caucasian society. Women raise their consciousness to a greater awareness of injustice and inequality. In a religious context, the theology of liberation speaks for the Third World, especially Latin America. One of the most important functions of theology, writes Gustavo Gutierrez, is "critical reflection, the fruit of a confrontation between the Word accepted in faith and historical praxis."[18] Pentecostals and evangelicals generally speak of breaking the bonds of worldliness.

Despite these stirrings of discontent with the world as it is, one may suggest that there are many people who are both unreflective and undisturbed, or at least their annoyances are more specific and personal. They may be only vaguely uneasy that the daily routine can best be endured with long stretches before the television or other frivolous ways of passing the tedium. If they feel a sense of entrapment, they may be quite content to leave things as they are. To be liberated from the grip of this utopian materialism allows us to seek the more worthwhile pursuits of human living; it helps to elevate us above and beyond the debilitating patterns of self-satisfaction.

Deprogramming Youth

It is not at all popular to suggest, as I do, that the whole process of socialization that we all experienced as young Americans was also a process of brainwashing, mind control, behavior modification. In other words, we were all programmed into our culture to accept the American way of life as the most natural and logical in the world.

The concept of brainwashing as a deliberate technique of indoctrination seems to have been applied originally to the Chinese communists who practiced thought control of the citizens.[19] This method seems to have a peculiarly Asiatic connotation, as when American prisoners of war were subjected to such treatment by the Viet Cong. The effect was that the individual abandoned his former loyalties, subscribed to a new and different ideology, and readily confessed the errors of his previous commitment. Originating in a non-Caucasian culture, it was seen as reprehensible and sinister, and "brainwashing" is the term then used to describe any psychological influence of which we disapprove. It becomes a logical charge to make against the Korean, the Reverend Sun Myung Moon.

While the term is now employed fairly loosely, it appears to remain uni-directional in the sense that the people who do the brainwashing are left-wingers, socialists desiring to introduce some foreign, un-American ideology. It is not popularly applicable to people who have adopted the right-wing ideology of Milton Friedman, Jerry Falwell, William Buckley, and similar conservatives. It is an interesting fact also that the switch from a religious to a secular ideology is not thought of as brainwashing, even though the individual was deprogrammed out of a church and reprogrammed into the secular culture. To the typical secular social scientist this would be the logical and reasonable step for the individual to take.

While religionists, pastors and parents bemoaned the defection of youthful believers from the church, the typical social scientist saw this as a demonstration of the expected evolution of secularization. The trend to secularism is seen as an inherent trait of developing civilization. It is chartered into the long-term program. There were other youth "problems" like drugs and delinquency, but the repudiation of religious values was not one of them. It seemed logical that American youth be rebellious about the rigid rules of the church, and that they seek to escape the religious traditions of their parents and family.

It appears that church leaders for the most part—especially in the mainline churches—miscalculated or misinterpreted the discontent of youth. Their response was an attempt to accommodate the church to the apparent desires of the people. If young people in particular were going secular, perhaps it was time then for the churches to move in a more liberal and secular direction. They began to liberalize the doctrines of both theology and morality. Even the Catholic Church, a traditional bulwark against the secularizing tendencies of our time, seemed to come to terms with modernity. The hope was that the fractious young Catholics could be retained, or regained, by the relaxations introduced in the Second Vatican Council. But it was too late. Robert Bellah opines that "the Catholic Church finally decided to recognize the value of the modern world just when American young people were beginning to find it valueless."[20]

In the light of recent pronouncements coming from the Vatican one might guess that Pope John Paul had heard Bellah's comment. As the church moved to modernize itself, many of the old-timers were saying that it is now much easier, more pleasant and relaxed, to practice Catholicism. Conservatives had watched the *Catholic Crisis* as seen by Thomas O'Dea[21] and the *Gathering Storm* predicted by Jeffrey Hadden.[22] What was thought to be an attractive readjustment for young people seems to have turned in upon itself. The generation that wanted to escape the harsh demands of religious mandates is replaced by a generation that now complains "everything is mixed up. You can't get a straight answer from the priests. You don't know what to believe anymore."

These observations lead us to a double generalization: young people are turning away, not only from the religious orthodoxy, but also from the secular orthodoxy. What is taken for granted as the proper acceptable urban modern culture has become unsatisfactory for youth. The objective system of traditional religious doctrine and practice has also become unpalatable for young people. This is a double kind of deprogramming that leaves the pious elders confused. They are glad to see their children turning away from secularism but they are unhappy to see them turning to a religious cult, which they see as quite alien to their own.

The terminology of brainwashing, of programming and deprogramming, may be new but the concept, when applied to religious conversion, is as old as the rivalry between peoples of different religious affiliations. Before the present era of ecumenical goodwill and interfaith understanding, the Jew who became a Christian was obviously coerced to do so. The young Protestant who converted to Catholicism was certainly bewitched by the wiles and deceptions of Rome. The so-called "fallen away" Catholic who joined a Protestant church had come under some evil influence that prevented him from thinking clearly. Ecumenism now absolves the switching of members among the large-scale American religions: the charge of brainwashing is brought only when people are "victimized" and "tricked" into joining some new religious cult, especially one with an Oriental flavor.

It seems quite legitimate then to say that the process of conversion from utopian materialism to transcendental religion is a process of deprogramming. The convert has repudiated the behavior patterns into which he had earlier been programmed, socialized, indoctrinated. The convert has called into serious question the values of his previous way of life, or at least some of them, and has raised his consciousness to prepare for change. "Conversion then," says DeMaria, "can be viewed as a method of re-education whereby one seeks to undo the unbalanced or unhealthy programming with which he or she has grown up."[23]

Factors of Conversion

It is characteristic of the secularist mentality that the religious act, the search for God, the religious conversion, must immediately be suspect. There must be "something wrong" with the individual who says that he or she has freely chosen to join a religious cult. There must have been delusion, seduction, trickery. Talking about young people who join cults, Levine offers the description "deliberately and carefully sought out and recruited by cult members, they are, and for some time remain, unaware that they have been selected as prospects by the proselytizers. The latter resort to every ruse imaginable to induce the young person to join the cult."[24]

This type of description of conversion to the Moonie cult is provided generally by three kinds of people. The first type are the people who have abandoned the group, are disgruntled about the experience for whatever reason, and are ready to blame others for their defection. "If the charge of mind control comes from ex-members, we have to ask how much of it is self-justification to explain away their once-ardent commitment to a cause they now reject."[25] They are in many ways similar to ex-Catholics who are ready to blame priests and nuns and other teachers for having subjected them to indoctrination in the catechism class of the parochial school.

The second type consists of the parents, many of whom have spent thousands of dollars in trying to retrieve their children from the clutches of the Unification Church. Berkeley Rice reports that "under the leadership of Rabbi Maurice Davis of White Plains, the national organization that has been formed of parents who have lost their children tries to locate them through the network of ex-members. If the parents wish, the organization puts them in touch with professional deprogrammers like Ted Patrick who may try to rescue the children for fees that can run to several thousand dollars. The deprogramming can be more brutal than any brainwashing the church may practice."[26]

The third type are the "expert" behavioral scientists who are ready and willing to assert that young people in their right minds simply do not choose to follow a leader like the Reverend Moon. Some tend to be contemptuous of such religious movements. C. Daniel Batson observed that "for the most part, mainstream psychology has treated the Unification Church and other psycho-religious cults with amused neglect."[27] The objective social scientist does not suffer the frustrations of ex-cultists or the disappointment of forsaken parents, but apparently cannot accept the fact that religious conversion may be a rational and intelligent experience.

In spite of the hysterical charges of trickery and seduction into the religious cult, it is safe to say that the overwhelming majority of young people who become cult members do so freely and deliberately, and for reasons that make sense to them. Anyone who wants to know what the reasons are has to face the fact that the motivation is both complex and multiple. A convert may express a single main reason for joining the religious group, but upon deeper self-analysis will reveal that several motives are present simultaneously. One of the favorite explanations was the so-called "deprivation" theory;[28] another was the assertion that only certain "personality types" are likely to succumb to the attractions of the new religion.[29]

Instead of relying on speculation concerning forms of deprivation or on arbitrary classifications of personality types, let us look at the reasons people give for decisions to affiliate religiously. In the earliest sociological study of the Moonies in America, Lofland described the seven steps, or stages, of the conversion model, from the perception of "considerable tension" to the involvement with "intensive interaction." The crucial stage seems to be that of "religious seekership," in the sense that all of these people "defined themselves as looking for an adequate religious perspective and had taken some action to achieve this end."[30]

We are talking here about a religious act, the effect of which is commitment to a religious group. The search for the sacred is, of course, above all a religious experience. If we speak in terms of needs and motives, we recognize here that the essence of religion is not fellowship, or theological doctrine, or a moral code. It is transcendental experience, a channel of contact with the sacred and the supernatural. The expression of this experience may be formalized in liturgies, spiritual devotion, cultic worship, but is in essence what Berger calls the "inductive" concept of religion. This is sharply distinguished from the deductive and reductive concepts of religion.[31]

Since motivation is multiple and complex, there are other supportive reasons why young people join a religious cult; and they are the same reasons why they join secular communes, country clubs and other primary groups. Probably the most frequently mentioned factor is simply the search for congenial fellowship.[32] Young people are attracted by the possibility of consorting with amiable people of their "own kind" who show concern for them. This is a response to the "love bombing" that is said to occur for the benefit of recruits to the Unification Church. Like novices in a religious order, they feel they are being treated with warmth and affection directed at them as special persons.

Another supplementary motive may be termed a search for freedom, the break away from the kinds of confining routines we have already described as the content of utopian materialism. This is something quite different from anarchy, or from the simplistic notion that young persons just want to do their "own thing." It seems safe to say that the behavioral conformity into which they had been socialized and indoctrinated had become distasteful, meaningless and valueless. Perhaps they are not sure why they rebel at the patterns of a sensate culture, except for the vague feeling that there has to be more to life than this.[33]

Still another subordinate motive appears to be in contrast to the search for freedom, but actually coincides with it. Young people turn away from the irrational demands of a sensate conformity and seek authoritative, dependable and reasonable norms. "They hunger for an authority that will simplify, straighten out, assure—something or somebody that will make their choices fewer and less arduous."[34] In other words, there is a need for an orderly system of norms and regulations on which youth can depend and to which they can give obedience. In his study of the Moon movement, Sontag reflected that "at least some of our young people today are looking for discipline, structure, strong parental figures, and they are willing to pour their commitment into a life of sacrifice and missionary zeal."[35]

Consequences of Religion

Sociologists should not be faulted if they are unable or unwilling to investigate the essential aspects of religion. By definition, and by the definition of their craft, they have to take a secular approach to the kind of data that are empirically verifiable. This is, of course, a limitation on the degree to which they can achieve a genuine understanding of a phenomenon that, by its very nature, has to include the relationship to the Divine, the Transcendent, the "Beyond." Yinger suggests that many modern intellectuals, including social scientists, have no parallel to this in their own lives. "A supernatural view of the world has become meaningless to them; they are repelled by a boastful and worshipful nationalism; they feel comfortable with a quiet kind of scientific secularism, motivated by idle curiosity with perhaps a nudge from a desire to help solve some human problem."[36]

There are some sociologists who profess a supernatural belief and who practice religion, but like the atheists or complete secularists, who maintain that religion is substantially false, they avoid the super-empirical and simply look at the relation between religion and society. Religion is studied, therefore, as a cultural and social phenomenon with man-made institutions and man-controlled organizations. The empirical and demonstrable data about religion are not derived from the sacred scriptures as the inspired word of God, nor is there any need to talk about divine revelation as the source of research data.

Unable to penetrate the core of religion, the sociologist must content himself with studying the consequences of religion. When we ask why young people join a religious cult we seem to be asking what religion does for them. What good is religion? What benefit do people get from it? Essentially for the individual, religion provides meaning in the search for the sacred; it satisfies the need for transcendent experience. Joining the religious group also responds to the need for companionship, for freedom, for orderliness.

The demonstrable fact is, of course, that religious groups and believing people continue to exist in our reputedly sensate materialistic society. They do hold theological beliefs; they do follow religious patterns of conduct. The functional assumption we make is that since these phenomena survive, since rational human beings embrace them, since they are empirically demonstrable, they must have some utility. People must find religion useful in the sense that it is satisfying some human and social need. This is not a proof for the truth of any religion. The non-functionalist might argue that religion could exist even if it were useless.

What we are saying is that the sociologists of religion tend to accept the notion that religion is functional for people in society; and they ask the questions: What precisely does religion do for people? What are the consequences of religion? What is its utility? The tendency then is also to bypass the question of the truth or falsity of institutionalized religion. At the same time, the anthropologist, Leonard Glick, proposes that "religion reflects, sustains, and legitimizes the social order," and he warns that we "should not labor with the misconception that our world is one in which religion is disappearing. For, to the contrary, the evidence is that new religions are arising all the time, that people do not respond to new problems by abandoning religion but by developing a new religion on the ruins of the old."[37]

The generalization that religion is useful, even necessary, for the survival of society rests on the functional theory that religion develops social solidarity among its adherents. Like all such neat theories, this one did not long go unchallenged. The utilitarian theory of integrative religion was questioned, researched, expanded, and refined. Robert Merton observed that the "spaceless and timeless generalizations about the integrative functions of religion are largely, although not of course entirely, derived from observation in non-literate societies."[38] Social critics who bemoan the general disintegration of Western civilization seem to feel that there are no remaining cohesive forces available to hold society together. Richard Fenn argues that secularization has undermined traditional bases of social authority and "dissolves traditional cultural wholes."[39]

If the sociologist no longer sees religion as an integrative force for society, the psychologist may argue that religion has certain therapeutic benefits for the individual. This, of course, continues the secular scientist's interest in religion as an instrumentality by and for human beings. It recalls Will Herberg's statement, that religion basically requires that human beings pay attention to God. Religion should not be seen primarily as a form of social welfare, as though it were meant to accommodate God to the wants of human beings. It is in this same vein that Robert Friedrichs remarked that people who believe in Biblical religion "deem at their core that faith rooted fundamentally in its utility is doctrinal heresy."[40]

The sociological reflection about religion, the functional theory about its cohesive quality, the concept of its social utility, will hardly promote a religious revival. These speculations are probably of little or no interest to the person who is moved by deep religious faith. With some scorn he may ask whether this is the best that can be said about religion: that it is useful for humanity. For the believer the point of importance is that religion has not disappeared: it has not been swallowed up into secularism.

The Religious Function

If we cut through all the secular, sociological and psychological theories about what religion "does" for people as individuals or in groups, we arrive at the believer's conviction that religious activity is an end in itself. The religious function is precisely what it appears to be: an encounter with truth, transcendence, the sacred. Regardless of what we say about it, or whether or not we think it is nonsense, the recruit to the Unification Church believes that he was created to respond to God's love "to be one in heart, will and action with God."[41] When we study the members of religious cults we have to take them seriously when the converts say they are in search of the sacred.

The thoroughgoing secularist is embarrassed by the concept of a personal relationship with God, and probably the majority of sociologists would scoff at the idea. They are reluctant to accept the fact that some people do somehow move out of the secular routine of the material world and actually experience the transcendent. This says nothing about theology, the study of which is an intellectual exercise, nor about the acceptance of a code of morality which guides human behavior. Neither theology nor ethics is at the core of religion: the encounter with the Holy.

In Christian history, the ascetics and the mystics who were recognized as saints prepared themselves for union with God through self-denial, fasting, and mortification. Their prayer was essentially a communication with God, perhaps more often in praise and thanksgiving than in supplication. The concept of the "presence of God" and of the "indwelling of the Holy Spirit" is traditional among the members of religious orders, in seminaries, monasteries and convents, and is a common recognition among the large numbers of lay people who go on spiritual retreats.

In other words, the basic religious experience, the personal relationship with God, is not a rare and newly discovered phenomenon by a few eccentrics in religious cults. Experience of being "born again" is almost routine among evangelical Protestants, and is now claimed by many charismatics across ecumenical lines, Catholics as well as mainline Protestants. Many Christians have made a public profession of acceptance of Jesus as personal savior, and in some mystical way feel that they are saved, or at least that they would like to be saved.

The Unification theologian, Young Oon Kim, refers to the Eucharist as the presence of Christ among Roman Catholics and Eastern Orthodox.[42] She quotes Karl Adam: "the faithful Catholic does not merely hope that Jesus will come to him. He know that he does. Holy Communion is a living intercourse with Jesus truly present."[43] She quotes also the Russian Orthodox Zernov: "The Eucharist is the meeting place between Jesus Christ and the Believer, personal, intimate, unique. It makes the Christian a new creature by elevating him into the Divine Presence."[44]

To say that one has had this religious experience once in a lifetime, or even several times, is not the same as describing the change that remains permanently after the conversion experience. The question, "have you been saved?" may refer to that one-time experience. the question, "are you saved?" seems to imply that the individual is in a permanent state of religiosity, remaining in the grace of God (to use old-fashioned language) until one loses God's friendship through sin. What the genuine religious convert realizes is that "life is different" as a result of the experience of conversion. This is willingly testified by persons who have had the "baptism in the Spirit" among Charismatics and Pentecostals. Many recovering alcoholics talk about the "spiritual awakening" that brought them new insights and a different level of behavior. The convert moves into an area that is sacred and supernatural. As Berger says, "the experience of the supernatural opens up the vista of a cohesive and comprehensive world. This other world is perceived as having been there all along, though it was not previously perceived and it forces itself upon consciousness as an undeniable reality, as a force bidding one to enter it."[45]

Parents who insist that their children have been mesmerized by Reverend Moon, or brainwashed by his followers, are willing to spend large sums of money to have their offspring deprogrammed. They obviously do not comprehend what a religious conversion means to the convert. Sontag sees them as young people who "are attracted by the demand for selfless devotion to a cause to usher in the new world of God's Kingdom now for all people."[46] Lofland pointed out that "a person who accepts the primary postulates and uses the everyday schema finds that reality is enormously transformed: everything becomes meaningful and understandable, more understandable perhaps than to those who rely on common sense."[47]

The secular skeptic who seeks solid rational proof of religious phenomena is not likely to accept the facts of conversion and the authentic experience of life's transformation. What we are talking about here is obviously a matter of religious faith. Psychologist Batson tends to deal sympathetically with the phenomenon of large numbers of young people who are joining the new religions. He suggests that his fellow psychologists, as secular skeptics, may well begin to examine their own value presuppositions which are threatened by the prevalence of religion.[48]

Footnotes

1 Daniel Bell, "The Return of the Sacred?" *British Journal of Sociology*, vol. 28, no. 4, 1977, p. 421
2 C. Daniel Batson, "Moon Madness: Greed or Creed?" pp. 218-225, in Irving L. Horowitz, ed., *Science, Sin and Scholarship*, Cambridge, MIT Press, 1978
3 Bryan Wilson, "The Return of the Sacred," *Journal for the Scientific Study of Religion*, vol. 18, no. 3, September 1979, pp. 268-280
4 John Lofland, *Doomsday Cult*, Englewood Cliffs, Prentice-Hall, 1966, p. 198
5 James T. Richardson, "Conversion, Brainwashing and Deprogramming," *The Center Magazine*, vol. 15, no. 2, pp. 18-24
6 Young Oon Kim, *Unification Theology and Christian Thought*, New York, Golden Gate, 1976, p. 40
7 See Rodney Stark and William Brainbridge, "Secularization and Cult Formation in the Jazz Age," *Journal for the Scientific Study of Religion*, vol. 20, December 1981, pp. 360-373
8 Robert Wuthnow, "The New Religions in Social Context," pp. 267-293, in Charles Glock and Robert Bellah, eds., *The New Religious Consciousness*, Berkeley, University of California Press, 1976
9 S.S. Acquaviva, *The Eclipse of the Sacred in Industrial Society*, New York, Harper and Row, 1979, p. 201
10 Sidney Hook, *Philosophy and Public Policy*, Carbondale, Southern Illinois University Press, 1979, sees secular humanism in opposition to organized religion
11 Paul Tillich, *Christianity and the Encounter of the World's Religions*, New York: Columbia University Press, 1963
12 In a document titled "Violence and Society," this utopian materialism is called a "sort of neopaganism with Christian cravings" and when it fails there result frustration, aggression and violence. See *Promotio Justitia*, no. 15, December 1979, pp. 162-171
13 *Ibid*, p. 165
14 Harvey Cox, *The Secular City*, New York: Macmillan, 1965, p. 20
15 The youthful counter-culture was seen as a "reaction against certain aspects of the rationalistic and utilitarian individualism of the recent phases of development of American society and industrial societies generally." Talcott Parsons, *Action Theory and the Human Condition*, New York, The Free Press, 1978, p. 320
16 Perhaps the most quoted early author of this phenomenon is William Graham Sumner, *Folkways*, Boston: Ginn, 1906. A kind of evolutionary determinism is associated with the "Cake of Custom"
17 Richard DeMaria, "A psycho-social Analysis of Religous Conversion," pp. 82-130, in M. Darrol Bryant and Herbert W. Richardson, eds., *A Time for Consideration: A Scholarly Appraisal of the Unification Church*, New York, Mellen Press, 1978
18 Gustavo Gutierrez, *A Theology of Liberation*, Maryknoll: Orbis Books, 1978, p. 79
19 See the study of Robert Jay Lifton, *Thought Reform and the Psychology of Totalism: A Study of Brainwashing in China*, New York, Norton, 1961, p. 3
20 Robert N. Bellah, "New Religious Consciousness and Crisis in Modernity," pp.

333-352, in Charles Glock and Robert Bellah, eds., *The New Religious Consciousness*, Berkeley, University of California Press, 1976

21 Thomas O'Dea, *The Catholic Crisis*, Boston, Beacon Press, 1968, was sure that there would remain "the Catholic sense of the importance of the spiritual, of the immediacy of God, and of the reality of the church mediating man's relation to God." p. xii

22 Jeffrey Hadden, *The Gathering Storm in the Churches*, Garden City, Doubleday, 1969, warns of the crisis of belief and authority in the Protestant clergy and sees it also "at work within Roman Catholicism." p. 5

23 R. DeMaria, *op cit.*, p. 89

24 Edward M. Levine, "Deprogramming Without Tears," *Society*, vol. 17, no. 3, March-April 1980, pp. 34-38: "Prospective members are completely unaware that they are being recruited or that they have unwittingly entered the first phase of what is actually a process of indoctrination."

25 Frederick Sontag, "Sun Myung Moon and the Unification Church: Charges and Responses," pp. 20-43, in Irving L. Horowitz, *op. cit.*

26 Berkeley Rice, "The Pull of Sun Moon," pp. 226-241, in Horowitz, *op. cit.* p. 239

27 C. Daniel Batson, "Moon Madness: Greed or Creed?" pp. 218-241, in Horowitz, *op. cit.*, p. 222

28 Five kinds of deprivation are related to membership in religious movements by Charles Glock, "The Role of Deprivation and the Origin and Evolution of Religious Groups," pp. 24-36, in Robert Lee and Martin Marty, ed., *Religion and Social Conflict*, New York, Oxford University Press, 1964

29 Even after admitting that both the definition and classification of personality are arbitrary, Kephart decides that people who join modern communes can be classified as the Parent-Haters, the Deepfeelers, the Non-Competitors, and the Borderliners. William Kephart, *Extraordinary Groups: The Sociology of Unconventional Life-Styles*, New York, St. Martin's Press, 1976, pp. 287-292

30 John Lofland, *op. cit.*, p. 44. Rosabeth Kanter, *Commitment and Community*, Cambridge, Harvard University Press, 1972, pointed out that nine successful communities, lasting from 33 to 184 years, she studied "began with some kind of religious base." A whole section of her book, pp. 111-125, treats of "Transcendence."

31 The deductive derives from a set of theological beliefs, while the reductive excludes the transcendent and makes religion a secular phenomenon. The advantage of the inductive option, says Berger, "is its openmindedness and freshness that usually comes from a non-authoritarian approach to questions of truth." Furthermore, "implied in this option is a deliberately empirical attitude, a weighing and assessing frame of mind." Peter Berger, *The Heretical Imperative*, Garden City, Doubleday, 1979, p. 63

32 This is mentioned first in a series of six "clusters" of reasons by Harvey Cox, *Turning East: Why Americans Look to the Orient for Spirituality*, New York, Simon and Schuster, 1977, p. 95

33 In a book about the youthful counter-culture which, despite its title, has nothing to do with religion, spirituality or God, Frank Musgrove, *Ecstasy and Holiness*, Bloomington, Indiana University Press, 1974, suggests that the problems of youth are rooted in "differences of values."

34 Harvey Cox, *op. cit.*, p. 98

35   Frederick Sontag, *op. cit.*, p. 209
36   J. Milton Yinger, *The Scientific Study of Religion*, New York; Macmillan, 1970, p. 11
37   Leonard Glick, "The Anthropology of Religion; Malinowski and Beyond," pp. 181-242, in Charles Glock and Phillip Hammond, eds., *Beyond the Classics: Essays in the Scientific Study of Religion*, New York; Harper and Row, 1973
38   Robert Merton, *Social Theory and Social Structure*, London; Macmillan, 1957, p. 28
39   Richard Fenn, *Toward a Theory of Secularization*, Storrs, University of Connecticut, 1978, p. 53. In his review of this book, N.J. Demarath thinks "Fenn is disappointed that a Durkheimian vision of an integrated society informed by a comprehensive symbol system is no longer apt, if it ever was." *Journal for the Scientific Study of Religion*, 18, September 1979, pp. 314-315
40   Robert Friedrichs, "An Articulate Witness," *Journal for the Scientific Study of Religion*, 18, 3, September 1979, pp. 313-314.
41   Frederick Sontag, *Sun Myung Moon and the Unification Church*, Nashville, Abington, 1977, p. 102
42   Young Oon Kim, *op. cit.*, 1976, pp. 296-299
43   Karl Adam, *The Spirit of Catholicism*, New York: Image Books, 1954, p. 198
44   N. Zernov, *Orthodox Encounter*, London: Clarke, 1961, p. 74
45   Peter Berger, *op. cit.*, p. 42
46   Frederick Sontag, *op. cit.*, p. 209
47   John Lofland, *op. cit.*, p. 197
48   C. Daniel Batson, *op. cit.*, p. 224, referring in particular to Donald Campbell, "Reforms as Experiments," *American Psychologist*, December 1975

IV Vocation to Marriage

By some odd coincidence, when I first encountered young members of the Unification Church most of them told me they had been Roman Catholics. I met them here and there, but mainly at the annual conferences of the International Cultural Foundation, and I always asked them where they came from and why they joined the Moonies. The young women and men who told me their current religious beliefs and practices did not pretend to represent a cross section of the membership. The fact is that the proportion of ex-Catholics in the Unification Church is higher than the Catholic percentage of the American population. This is true also of ex-Jews who are now Moonies. At any rate, these young people are alert, articulate, enthusiastic and, above all, they have a sense of vocation.

They are quite ready to say that they have a "calling;" that they are beckoned by God for a life of dedication to his service. This has been a conversion experience, a "spiritual awakening" that now points their lives in the direction of the divine will of the Father. As I came to know them better, and also interviewed others who are now members of the Krishna movement, Assemblies of God, Pentecostals and fundamentalist groups, I have a hunch that a generation ago these young Catholics would have followed their vocation into the seminary, the monastery and the convent. They would have become monks and nuns, and perhaps even mother superiors and monsignors. I have a suspicion that they are the answer to the plaintive cry of the bishops and religious provincials: where have all the church vocations gone?

The so-called "vocation shortage" is a contemporary problem that seems peculiar to the Catholic Church. Most of the mainline Protestant churches appear to have an abundance of clergy and even a surplus of prospective ministers now in the seminary.[1] In their case this is a tight "job market" for clergy positions, especially in those large denominations where the lay membership is not increasing, or is even on the decline.[2] On the other hand, the Catholic church authorities have been bemoaning the "vocation crisis" for more than a decade. The decline in vocations to the priesthood, sisterhood and brotherhood began shortly after the close of the Second Vatican Council, and was noticed not only in the exodus of many religious professionals, but also in the smaller number of young women and men aspiring to full-time church ministry.[3]

While it is true that the Moonie has a lay vocation, it is thought of as something more than Luther's universal vocation of the laity, who taught that everyone has a calling from God, and that vocation centered on whatever job, occupation, or activity a person does in everyday life. A similar concept is that of Catholic Action in the so-called "lay apostolate," confirmed and promoted by the Second Vatican Council. The Church is the People of God, and the lay people are encouraged not only to participate in the internal operation of the Church but they also "exercise a genuine apostolate by their activity on behalf of penetrating and perfecting the temporal sphere of things through the spirit of the gospel."[4] In all of history there have been holy people, sometimes formally affiliated with organized religion, sometimes not, who experienced a special kind of relationship with God. The laity are the great majority of all people in all religions, and one may well assume that the great majority of saintly men and women throughout history were also lay persons. The converts to the Unification Church, however, give more than ordinary laic dedication to their calling.

One of the more inflammatory charges against the Unification community is that membership is disruptive of family life. The new converts leave home and family, brothers and sisters, to dedicate themselves entirely to the religious calling. Parents sometimes charge that their children have been "brainwashed." Similar charges were at times brought against Catholic religious orders that lured a daughter to the convent or a son to the novitiate. Spiritual counselors have long said that God's call must be obeyed even if parents are in opposition. Some Catholic parents have even forbidden their teen-age children to attend charismatic prayer meetings lest they be drawn too frequently out of the family circle and the "normal" activities of youth.

Moonies and Novices

The process of becoming a full-fledged member of the Unification Church is in some ways similar to that which a Catholic youth experiences on entering the novitiate of a religious order. Life there is regulated, disciplined and goal-oriented. You give up your worldly aspirations and your worldly goods and commit yourself to the ideals of the organization. No drugs, no alcohol, no sex, no money, few decisions and few worries. You put yourself under spiritual direction and you develop a loyalty to the religious congregation, its program, its philosophy, its leaders.

In both cases the individuals feel a call to a deeper spirituality, a closer union with God and a more meaningful prayer life, than they had previously experienced. They also develop an enthusiasm for the church's teachings that encourages them to share the good news of salvation with others. Catholics who have converted to the Unification Church feel that their new religion has a universal concern, a program for embracing the whole mass of humanity, while they think that Catholicism tends to focus its spirituality on a predominantly personal relationship with God. One of them, who likes ecumenical jargon, said that the Catholic Church is "culture-bound" and does not make much progress with non-Europeans and non-Westerners.

Stereotypes are almost always expressed when people discuss differences in religion, race and ethnicity. Judgments about the lack of universality of the Catholic ideology are as erroneous as judgments about the use of brainwashing in the recruitment of Moonie adherents. Every church faces this problem: how does one correct misinformation? Every church recognizes that the truth about itself is very different from the false perceptions that others have of it. The anti-defamation league of B'nai B'rith is the prime example of organized effort to sift truth from error in the minds of non-Jews. Nevertheless, prejudices have a life on their own and are effective guides of behavior, as in the case of young Catholics who carry misperceptions of their church as "reasons" for switching their allegiance to another religion.

From the point of view of prospective lifelong vocation the big difference between the Catholic novice and the Moonie recruit is that the Catholic religious order is guiding you to a career of permanent celibacy. Personal holiness lies in that direction. In contrast, the totally committed member of the Unification community is being prepared for marriage and family. The individual is spiritually incomplete until joined to a spouse in holy matrimony, and is participating in a blessed family. Single persons who are converted to the church—most of them are in their mid-20s—soon learn the theological and spiritual importance of family life, for which they are destined. With rare exceptions, there is not much future for a celibate among the "core" members of the Unification Church.

Young people who "join the family" take up residence in a Unification center with other male and female members, strictly segregated by sex. Frederick Sontag calls it a "coed monasticism."[5] They develop a family relationship looking across sex lines at brothers and sisters. There is a spiritual kinship of *agape*, close-knit camaraderie and group support within the residence. Selfishness is a serious personal fault. Christian love is the key word, and this collective relationship can be harmonious only if it is God-centered. They spend a relatively short period of time at the training center, and then travel in smaller groups of eight to ten in mobile fundraising teams (MFT) in which they also "witness" to their faith to new prospective recruits, or "spiritual children."

While novices and trainees in Catholic religious orders now tend also to do a limited amount of "field work" in certain apostolic ministries, they obviously go out together in unisex groups. The novitiates, scholasticates and houses of study of religious orders never combine the sexes. They are either exclusively male communities which develop a kind of fraternal solidarity among the members, or exclusively female communities which are characteristic of the Catholic sisterhoods. Seminarians who are studying for the diocesan priesthood tend to develop a somewhat loose bond of fellowship among themselves. They do not pronounce the three vows of poverty, chastity and obedience as in the typical community of the religious order or congregation. Traditionally, Catholics were in their teens when seeking admission to seminaries and novitiates. This early age of entrance differs from the practice of the Unification Church where "minors," or teenagers, are not admitted to full membership. Catholic minor seminaries, which are the equivalent of college preparatory academies, have gradually decreased in numbers of students, and many have ceased to exist. In other words, the average age at entrance to both diocesan seminaries and religious orders has moved to the early twenties and is beginning to resemble that of the neophyte Unificationists. A significant change has occurred, however, in the fact that increasing numbers of females are now studying theology and aspiring for academic degrees in Catholic seminaries. Women professors, though in small numbers, have been hired to the faculties of these seminaries.[6]

The Value of Chastity

While there has been much discussion about the ordination of women to the Catholic priesthood, and about the relaxation of the law of celibacy for the Catholic clergy, there appears little likelihood that any significant changes will be allowed in these centuries-old traditions. The Unification Church, in contrast, maintains a theological seminary at Barrytown, New York, where both brothers and sisters are in attendance as students. This theological training does not lead to ordination of either male or female students, nor is the seminary a normal experience for the great majority of the young membership. Most members obtain their training for the ministry of witnessing, or evangelizing, in occasional retreats and seminars, and in actual day-to-day experience "on the road."

While the prospective Catholic church functionary prepares for life-long celibacy, the youthful Unificationist goes through a period of strict voluntary celibacy preparatory to marriage. It is a serious mandate of Unification theology that members practice the virtue of chastity in premarital celibacy as well as during married life. In other words, the sins of sex, whether fornication before marriage or adultery in marriage, are the most serious kinds of immorality among the church members. Michael Mickler calls this "vocational singleness," and says that "for core members, primary thrust is toward religious experience, that is, the variety of ways one might experience God's heart. In this setting, traditional vocational norms of poverty, chastity and obedience are integrated with what might otherwise be viewed as 'non-vocational' aspects of single life within the church."[7]

It should be noted that the strict rule of pre-marital chastity is a preparation for marriage, but it is also tied in with the practice of poverty and obedience. The young Moonies allow themselves to be directed in the work they do, the place they reside, the people with whom they associate. This is the virtue of obedience. Similarly, they practice the virtue of poverty. One young professional woman, accustomed to having an income of spendable money, said, "one of the hardest things I experienced is in not having ready money at hand." The receipts from fundraising are turned over to the church; great care is taken not to "waste" anything; food is adequate but frugal; necessary expenditures are kept to a minimum.

"Within the Unification context, singleness is seen as foundational for family life, not only spiritually (that is, in the development of parental heart), but also structurally in that one's spiritual children are the foundation for one's physical children."[8] From a pragmatic perspective also, the several years experience of celibacy allows the young Moonies freedom to pursue the work of the church as well as their own spiritual formation. Paul's oft-quoted message to the Corinthians is that the unmarried persons, men or women, can be fully dedicated to the Lord's work.[9] They are free of the worldly worries that seem characteristic of married life. Unlike the permanently vowed Catholic celibate, the young Unificationist maintains temporary and deliberate celibacy in preparation for the vocation of marriage.

The desire for both sanctification and full-time service of God motivated the original Christian cenobites to remove themselves from worldly concerns. The normal practice, however, of the apostles and their successors, popes, bishops and priests, was that they continued for centuries to marry and beget children. It is a fact that a married man, Adrian II, was elected Pope as late as the ninth century. The earliest attempt to impose celibacy was at the Spanish Council of Elvira (c300) which required absolute continence for its clergy. Clergy marriages were in many places discouraged and considered illicit, but it was not until the Lateran Councils (1123 and 1139) that they were officially declared invalid. Even then the restrictive regulation was not easily enforced. On the other hand, the voluntary "religious" vocation—to distinguish diocesan from regular clergy, and communities of sisters from other kinds of female groupings—evolved gradually from the monks of the desert in the early centuries. It was Saint Benedict, however, in the year 535, who "regularized" the community life of celibates, monasteries for males, convents for females. He is known as the father of monasticism.

The training schedule in the Unification Church is a temporary and deliberate program of celibacy which is seen as a serious preparation for chaste marriage. It is during this "premarital apprenticeship" that the young Moonie approximates the "first blessing" of Unification theology, the development of a spiritual, virtuous, sinless relationship with God. "According to Unification reasoning, it is only by giving one's undivided love and attention to God and to the service of humanity—and this entails at least for a time a postponement of sexual relationships, which for the Moonies equals postponement of marriage—that one can develop the virtues upon which the practice of true family depends."[10]

The Call to Marriage

One searches in vain through the Patristic writers and conventional theologians of earlier centuries for a concept of the marriage vocation that parallels the celibate vocation. Among the Jews who provided the pattern for the adult married women and men who converted to the early Christian community, there appeared to be no religious content to the marital ceremony. "The idea of celebrating these marriages with a separate church ceremony, distinct from the normal civil marriage celebrated in the family or the immediate social circle, did not at first come to mind. Christians did much the same as their non-Christian fellows, the Greeks and the Romans, and later the Germanic, Frankish, Celtic, and other peoples."[11]

The early Christians were culturally Jewish and they apparently saw no reason for introducing religious rituals into their marriage ceremonies. Nevertheless, the vocation to marriage was seen as a religious obligation that was binding on both Jew and Christian. "Indeed marriage is seen in Jewish tradition as a sacred act, and the Hebrew word for it, *kiddushin*, comes from the Hebrew root, *holy*." As a matter of fact, marriage was obligatory among a people who had neither sympathy nor understanding of vows of virginity. For every Jewish youth "marriage is both the climax and the threshold. From birth on, every step is directed with an eye to the hupa (marriage canopy) and if that goal were missed, life itself would seem to be bypassed."[12] Since marriage was the natural and customary anticipation of all Jewish youth, it was probably seen by new Christians also as a response to the divine plan for humanity. The "vocation" to marriage then would have been deemed a universal invitation, even a mandate from heaven.

This cultural pressure to marry was probably as strong among the early Christians as among their Jewish contemporaries. It is a historical fact that the great majority of early Christians viewed marriage as the normal, customary pattern of adult life. The Talmud includes the statement that "he who has no wife lives without joy, without blessing, and without goodness." Saint Paul praises marital unity as similar to the union of Christ and the Church, "a man will leave his father and mother, and unite with his wife, and the two shall be one."[13] This continued to be the case in subsequent centuries, although there are occasional references to individual "consecrated virgins." In spite of the reverence and appreciation for marriage among the Christians, Theodore Mackin notes a "surprising lack of difference between early Christian marriages and those of their pagan neighbors." The secular ceremony of marriage was still recognized by the Synod of Elvira in 306, which accepted that Christian marriages were celebrated the same way as those of pagans. "There was in fact no distinct Christian wedding ceremony obligatory on all members of the Church for the first nine centuries of Christian history.[14]"

Aside from the teaching that virginity held a spiritual superiority over marriage there developed a consistent Manichee crusade against the "evils" of marriage, especially intercourse and procreation. While the orthodox doctrine maintained that celibacy is the more perfect state of life, the early Patristic writers were forced to argue that there is nothing morally wrong with marriage. Clement of Alexandria even admitted that "marriage, if used properly, is a way of salvation for all: priests, deacons and laymen." Augustine rejected as ridiculous "the opinion of some of his contemporaries that Adam's and Eve's sin was their having intercourse for the first time and prematurely against God's will, since it is clear in Genesis that they had intercourse for the first time only after their sin."[15]

Since consecrated virginity and celibacy were esteemed as a "higher" calling than marriage, one gets the impression that the great theologians of the church gave only reluctant approval of marriage as a God-given vocation. Preoccupation with the moral "dangers" of carnal concupiscence has never been far from the minds of Christian moralists, a general attitude that may help to explain the warnings that the expressions of sexuality, even in marriage, must be kept carefully under control. The Manichee heresy reappears in various guises, as the Albigensians and the Cathars who condemned marriage and sexuality as moral degradation. The moral rigorism of the Jansenists condemned the pleasureable use of marriage and continued its negative influence into the early twentieth century.[16]

Against the heretics and rigorists who argued that sexual intercourse is sinful, even within the state of matrimony, the church officially and over the centuries defended the legitimacy of the conjugal bond. The response of the Lateran Council in 1139 was to excommunicate the Cathars who derogated marriages that were held in honorable approval by the church and community. Even then, however, the sacramental character of marriage had not been clarified. To off-set the Manichee teachings of the times, the Synod of Verona in 1184 issued an official document that declared marriage for the first time a sacrament, "placed on the same footing as baptism, the eucharist, and the sacrament of penance."[17] Even when sacramental marriage had been recognized as a source of divine grace and an effective help to salvation, it was still treated in scholastic thought and textbooks as a refuge from concupiscence, a *remedium* for Christians who were not able to live in sexual continence.

More recently, with the promulgation of papal encyclicals, moral counsel was commonly given on the subject of Christian marriage, as in the *Dum Multa* (1902) of Leo XIII and the *Casti Connubii* (1930) of Pius XI. It was not, however, until 1956 that Pope Pius XII solemnly declared that the theological concept of vocation may be applied to the state of marriage. Sattler recognizes the evolution of doctrine and remarks that "in the emerging Christian concept, marriage is the vocation of a baptized man and woman to that state, consecrated by the Sacrament of Matrimony, devoted to the service of new life in Christ, which involves the specific spiritual perfection of the spouses as a way of life."[18]

Even more recently the Fathers of the Second Vatican Council confirmed and clarified the exalted vocation of marriage and its divine origin. "The Creator of all things has established the conjugal partnership as the beginning and basis of human society." This means that "Christian husbands and wives are cooperators in grace and witnesses of faith on behalf of each other, their children and all others in their household.'[19] In another document the council de-clared that "God Himself is the author of matrimony," and affirmed that "the intimate partnership of married life and love has been established by the Creator and qualified by His laws. It is rooted in the conjugal covenant of irrevocable personal consent. Hence, by that human act whereby spouses mutually bestow and accept each other, a relationship arises which by divine will and in the eyes of society is a lasting one."[20]

Mandate from Heaven

The marriage chances for a Moonie are limited in one direction and expanded in another. The member is not permitted to marry outside the church family; that is, the spouse must be a fellow adherent of the Unification Church. There is no such thing as a "mixed religious" marriage for a Unificationist. This is the same strict rule that governs the marriage of Salvation Army officers and the mate selection of Mormons and of Israeli Jews. It was the same rule against mixed marriages which has gradually lost its effectiveness in the Catholic Church. Any member who wants to marry outside the Unification community has obviously misunderstood the central significance of sharing religious values in lifelong fidelity.

On the other hand, there is a broadening of marriage opportunities in the Unification approval of "mixed" marriages across racial and ethnic lines. The conventional pattern of marrying someone of your own nationality and social status, especially of your own race, is widely disregarded in this religious movement. At the mass wedding in New York's Madison Square Garden in 1982, more than one-third of the couples were interracial. The large Oriental membership, especially of Koreans and Japanese, makes available to Caucasians a prospect of marriage partners that they would not ordinarily have. Sharing the same religious beliefs and practices provides a communal value that transcends racial, ethnic and class preferences.

Marriage is a serious, holy and obligatory "sacrament" for which lengthy preparation is required. It is a mandate from heaven which does not allow the alternative of bachelorhood or singleness. It is reminiscent of the earlier Mormon dictum that "no man will be exalted in the celestial kingdom without a wife and no woman without a husband."[21] In the spiritual preparation for this ceremony the stages of formation and growth precede the stage of perfection, which is the "first blessing." It is clear that Moonies do not rush into marriage, but then there is no need to hurry. They have assurances that Reverend Moon will find the preordained life partner for them. The concept of "arranged" marriages is alien to young Americans, although it has been an accepted pattern for most of humanity for most of human history. Members have an abiding trust in Mr. Moon as the voice of God for them. One recently engaged man remarked: "You try to have confidence in your prayer life that God knows what is best for you, that He will work through Reverend Moon to suggest the proper match for you."

Preoccupation with the dating game, the hazards of flirty infatuation and the excitement of romantic love are avoided in the custom of arranged marriages. The attraction to each other is spiritually motivated and spiritually sustained. They are putting God's will, as expressed to them by their religious leader, before their own. As in everything else they do, the primary motive in preparing for marriage is to follow the will of God. "We both love God more than we love each other; and that's the way it ought to be, and it's the only way we can hope to have a God-centered family."

The secular and contemporary American family way of "getting engaged" is a very private agreement in which parents, relatives and friends must not dare to interfere. There may be a party celebrated, and even some gift-garnering "showers" after the engagement has been announced. The custom of a religious and solemn engagement before friends and in the presence of a priest was in vogue among Catholics for a while when the liturgical movement was young. The engagement ceremony for members of the Unification Church is a sacred and public event, and is celebrated by numerous couples simultaneously. When the couple shares a cup of wine on that occasion they are establishing a spiritual lineage that is permanent and indissoluble. "At that point the commitment is binding and eternal. Through the taking of the wine and participation in the ceremony, sins are forgiven and rebirth occurs. The couple is then offered to God as newly created beings, pure and free of past sins."[22]

The engagement that is blessed by God and approved by the church is not primarily of the flesh. It allows no liberties of a sexual nature. The consummation of the marriage, living together and "starting a family" are also governed by religious obedience. In the spirit of self-sacrifice and as an indemnity for the sins of the world, all couples abstain from sex for forty days after marriage, and in most instances they are sent on separate missions to different parts of the world before settling down to family life. This is no ordinary marriage. It is the ritualistic channel to salvation; it is the God-ordained "blessed" couple fulfilling their spiritual vocation.

The primary purpose of marriage in the Unification Church is to give joy and glory and honor to God, and the primary purpose of sexual coition is the procreation of children. Spiritual perfection cannot be achieved in self-centered and lonely celibacy. Even after receiving the second blessing of matrimony, the spouses seek perfection through experiencing the three stages of love in the God-centered family: the mutual love of wife and husband, the love of parents for children and the love of children for parents. The family is the foundation for understanding the love of God. To become "true parents" and to populate the earth with spiritually perfect individuals are to help create the Kingdom of God and to bring salvation to a sinful world.

The time has now come for the members of the Unification Church to establish perfect families in love and justice and unity, which in turn will unify all races, all nations, all religions. The divine scheme of love and family is laid out in the "four-position foundation," which appears to be a cumbersome theological and relational formula. The four positions are: God, husband, wife, child. The pure and perfect relationship with God helps to establish the perfect relationship between husband and wife, and then between parents and children.[23]

The spiritual and physical Kingdom of God, the total redemption that God intended in sending the messiah, will allegedly be achieved by the ever-expanding network of such God-centered families.

Family Indemnity

When Catholics talked about "following a vocation" they almost always meant the kind of life that required permanent celibacy, whether in the diocesan or religious priesthood, as well as among religious sisters and brothers. This was the "more perfect" spiritual path to one's own eternal salvation. It was primarily a personal relationship with God, which was also to provide availability in the ministry to all other children of God. There was always room, of course, for the vocation of marriage, but it was at best a second-level and risky pathway to God. The Moon people have turned this around. If you really want to do God's will, if you want the higher vocation, if you want the life of spiritual perfection, you marry and have children.

Unification theology provides the rationale for the emphasis on family life. God created Adam and Eve with a potential to both spiritual and physical perfection. "The purpose of creation is to give joy to God," writes theologian Herbert Richardson.[24] The first great joy for our original parents was meant to be the experience of God's love and the attainment of individual perfection. The establishment of a saintly family meant that God's love would be shared in the second great joy. Ultimately then, the sharing of God's love with the whole universe fulfills God's plan for his kingdom on earth.

According to the theology of *Divine Principle,* the revealed scripture of the Unification Church, God intended Adam and Eve to marry and have perfect children who would populate his physical and spiritual kingdom. This intention was frustrated when Eve was sexually seduced by the archangel Lucifer, committing the original sin of adultery and causing the spiritual fall of mankind. Her impurity was passed on in premature and illicit intercourse with Adam, causing the physical fall of man.[25] Later, God sent Jesus to redeem humanity from sin. He accomplished his spiritual mission, but was killed before he could marry and father a new race of perfect children (in whom there would be no original sin). Our first parents threw away God's love; Jesus was prevented from completing the redemptive mission on which his heavenly Father had sent him.

Conventional Christian theologians, as represented by the Commission on Faith and Order of the National Council of Churches of Christ, have found these teachings rampant with heresy.[26] Their critique of Unification theology concludes that the Unification Church is not a Christian Church, nor do its doctrines reflect a "continuity with the Christian faith." Theologians, of course, are not expected to analyze the sociological consequences of church doctrine even while the pragmatic sociologist recognizes that the Moonies seem to have come upon a family program that "works." While marriage counselors and parish clergy are wringing their hands over the breakdown of modern family life, the Unification Church proposes a solution. The God-centered family is not merely a nice slogan or a spiritual ideal suggested by the church leaders. It is the essential core of community among the faithful of the church. It is also a deeply motivated system for restoring marital fidelity and family stability to modern society.

One need not be an expert moral theologian to recognize the notable shift that has been occurring in the marital and family values of American society. Many secularists see this change as an expression of personal freedom, an opportunity for self-actualization. Spiritually sensitive people, however, see it as a decline in personal morality as well as a disregard for community needs and values. In either case these changing patterns of behavior reflect a significant restructuring of the family system that has long been integral to western civilization. The evidence on shifting marital and familial values is drawn from fairly reliable statistics on human behavior and attitudes: premarital sex, venereal disease, teenage pregnancies, abortion, pornography, infidelity, divorce.

The religious values of the Judeo-Christian tradition have generally been supportive of marital fidelity and family stability. Church leaders, pastors and preachers often express concern that these values are being destroyed. Yet in some instances the churches have "relaxed" their doctrines and practices to accommodate the behavior patterns and preferences of their adherents. Moral concessions have been made in the matter of trial marriage and divorce, birth prevention and even abortion. Organized religion in the mainline churches has been relatively unsuccessful in stemming the downward curve. Unification leaders stand fast against sinful, selfish sex—the basis and cause of all immorality—and they are not about to join those "progressive theologians" who are trying to "develop an ethic of developmental sexuality and personality growth that changes the focus away from the negative control mechanisms (sex as sinful, immoral behavior) and toward greater concern for the integrity of the individuals."[27]

Whatever one may say in criticism of the Unification Church as a social and religious movement and even as a purveyor of theological heresy, one has to recognize its sytematic program for the restoration of "old-fashioned" morality, its emphasis on chastity before marriage, prayerful preparation for marriage, a readiness to accept guidance in the choice of a spouse, marital love reflective of love of God, transmission of spiritual perfection to children. The Unification Church insists that religion is the moral bond of family solidarity and that the family is the moral basis of society. Family, religion and community are integrally related, and Unification ideology emphasizes the centrality of the family in maintaining a religious culture and in transmitting a spiritual tradition.

Footnotes

1 Jackson Carroll and Robert Wilson, *Too Many Pastors?* New York, Pilgrim Press, 1980
2 Carl Dudley, *Where Have All Our People Gone?* New York, Pilgrim Press, 1979
3 Joseph H. Fichter, "Catholic Church Professionals," The *Annals* of the American Academy of Political and Social Sciences, 1970, vol. 387, pp. 77-85
4 *Apostolicam Actuositatem,* Decree on the Apostolate of the Laity, article 2
5 Frederick Sontag, *Sun Myung Moon,* Nashville, Abingdon, 1977, p. 28
6 A warning has been issued from the Vatican, declaring that there are to be no females, either as students or faculty, at Catholic seminaries
7 Michael L. Mickler, "Crisis of Single Adults: An Alternative Approach," pp. 161-173, in Gene G. James, ed., *The Family and the Unification Church,* New York, Rose of Sharon, 1983
8 *Ibid.,* p. 171
9 I Corinthians, 7/32-34
10 Tom Walsh, "Celibacy, Virtue, and the Practice of True Family in the Unification Church," in Gene G. James, *op. cit.,* pp. 139-159
11 E. Schillebeeckx, *Marriage: Secular Reality and Saving Mystery,* London, Sheed and Ward, 1965, p. 3. It was only in the fourth century that a "marriage service" was introduced, including God's blessing as used for marriage in the synagogue. *Ibid.,* p. 25
12 M. Zborowski and E. Herzog, *Life Is with People,* New York, Schocken, 1952, p. 290

13 Ephesians, 5/32
14 Theodore Mackin, *What Is Marriage?* New York, Paulist Press, 1982, p. 78
15 *Ibid.,* p. 132
16 See Nigel Abercrombie, *The Origins of Jansenism,* Oxford, Clarendon Press, 1936, pp. 139f
17 E. Schillebeeckx, *op. cit.,* p. 165
18 H.V. Sattler, "Marriage as a Vocation," pp. 265-267, in *New Catholic Encyclopedia,* vol. ix, New York, McGraw-Hill, 1967. See also Pius XII, *Sedes Sapientiae,* article 48
19 *Apostolicam Actuositatem,* Decree on the Laity, article 11
20 *Gaudium et Spes,* Decree on the Church Today, article 48
21 Darwin L. Thomas, "Family in the Mormon·Experience," pp. 267-288, in William D'Antonio and Joan Aldous, eds., *Families and Religions,* Beverly Hills, Sage, 1983
22 Hugh and Nora Spurgin, "Blessed Marriage in the Unification Church," pp. 121-137, in Gene G. James, ed., *The Family and the Unification Church,* New York, Rose of Sharon Press, 1983
23 *Divine Principle,* "The Four-Position Foundation," New York, Holy Spirit Association, 1977, fifth edition, p. 32
24 Herbert Richardson, "Lecture at Barrytown," pp. 290-317, in M. Darrol Bryant and Herbert Richardson, eds., *A Time for Consideration,* New York, Mellen Press, 1978
25 "Fall of Man," pp. 67-97, in *Divine Principle,* New York, Holy Spirit Association, 1977, fifth edition
26 See the official study document "Critique of the Theology of the Unification Church as Set Forth in Divine Principle," pp. 102-118, in Irving Horowitz, ed., *Science, Sin and Scholarship,* Cambridge, MIT Press, 1978. Further critical comments by sociologists were edited by Roger O'Toole, "Symposium on Scholarship and Sponsorship," *Sociological Analysis,* vol. 44, no. 3, Fall, 1983, pp. 177-225
27 William V. D'Antonio, "Family Life, Religion, and Societal Values and Structures," pp. 81-140, in William V. D'Antonio and Joan Aldous, eds., *Families and Religions,* Beverly Hills, Sage, 1983

V Structure of the Church

When Sun Myung Moon began preaching to a handful of followers in 1946 in Pyung-Yang, Korea, he "tried to establish a secure foundation for God's new dispensation," but he apparently had no thought or plan for founding a worldwide church. He felt called upon to preach the word of God, to make converts to the message of salvation, and to send disciples out to other countries. His most articulate theologian, an English-speaking Korean woman, Young Oon Kim, was his first missionary to the United States in 1959.[1] She was more intent on preaching Moon's new revelation than in working out plans for a religious organization. From a sociological perspective one may say that the Unification Church was not built according to some carefully planned blueprint but that it gradually evolved a social structure in the course of its growth and experience.

The basic doctrines of the Unificationists emerged from the revelations of Sun Myung Moon and were later systematized in the now sacred book, *Divine Principle,* by Young Oon Kim. The beliefs and practices of the movement originate with the revered founder, who was born in Korea in 1920. Although he is commonly addressed as "Reverend" he has never been ordained to the ministry in any of the Christian churches. Although the book is a revision of Biblical accounts of God's relation with humanity, Reverend Moon is not conversant with the original Biblical languages, is not a professional theologian, nor an acknowledged scripture scholar. Church historian Warren Lewis says that his "Christianity is a composite of the results of Presbyterian missionary preaching, Methodist holiness, and Pentecostal charisma. To this he adds his own reading of the Bible and his experiences with Jesus Christ. According to Moon,

Jesus first appeared to him on a Korean mountainside on Easter morning in 1936, when he was 16 years old. Jesus told Moon that he was to complete the Messianic task of bringing about the Kingdom of Heaven on earth."[2]

The sociological analyst makes no attempt either to sanctify the founder of the Unification Church nor to discredit him or his interpretation of *Heilsgeschichte*. The Apostles' Creed, professed by large numbers of practicing Christians, differs considerably from the series of twelve theological beliefs in the proclamation signed by 38 students at the Barrytown Seminary on October 14, 1976. There is, however, sociological significance in this Unificationist Creed that is meant to promote "the unity of Christian theologies, Christian denominations, and Christian churches, to accomplish an interfaith movement."[3] This ambitious purpose necessarily requires some viable form of social organization, a systematic cooperation between the leaders and their followers and a set of functional relations among the members. The Unificationists insist that their organization is something more than a conventional church structure. For want of a better term we may say that they are attempting to build a familial-ecclesial way of life.

The Moonie Collectivity

Sociological concepts like cult, sect, denomination are loosely used in varying descriptions of this religious organization which formally calls itself the Holy Spirit Association for the Unification of World Christianity. Its beginnings were interrupted by the Korean War when Moon and some of his followers were imprisoned by the Communists in the north, but were later freed by the United Nations soldiers in 1950. He began preaching again in 1951 at Pusan, but in 1953 moved to Seoul, the capital of the Republic of Korea. The official date of the founding of this Association was 1954, when it was recognized by the civil authorities and certified as a legal social organization. Since that time it has generally been known everywhere as a church.

John Lofland, who later studied the group on the West Coast, interpreted it as a deviant millenarian sect and an "ideological splinter group," although in reality the Moonie movement had not separated from a parent denominational church as is the case with numerous Protestant sects. The sect is often interpreted as a movement in protest against the parent church, and the cult in protest against the larger society. In the popular American media any religious group that looks strange and different and does not conform to the common perception of Judeo-Christian traditions is labeled a cult.[4] Even after the group has evolved into a highly organized *ecclesia*, like the Unification Church, it is still erroneously called a cult by columnists, newscasters and even some social scientists.

The Holy Spirit Association is clearly not a cult if we accept the common sociological criteria for defining a cult as formulated by Ernst Troeltsch as a category of mysticism and elaborated by Howard Becker. From this perspective, the cult is a small, relatively unstructured group of believers seeking personal ecstatic experience under the guidance of a charismatic leader. Their beliefs and practices have not yet become institutionalized. One may well suggest that the informal and devout primary group of disciples surrounding Jesus were an incipient religious cult. I have argued elsewhere that the Catholic Charismatics, who remain within the large parent church, could be termed a cult rather than a sect.[5] These descriptions, however, are inappropriate for the American Moonies.

While the Unification Church is neither a sect nor a cult, its design and purpose allow it to fit the definition of a religious movement. Killian points out that a social movement grows out of the unrest and dissatisfaction of people who seek social reform and want to promote a better system of living. It is a "collectivity acting with some continuity to promote or resist a change in the society or group of which it is a part."[6] The Moonies interpret themselves as an evangelical movement, working for the salvation of individuals and society, transforming the world according to the divine revelation and in anticipation of the Second Coming. The members are deeply convinced that they are participating in the dynamics of world reform, based on the prophetic nature of the religious revelations that Reverend Moon feels mandated to teach his followers and all the world. Organized teams of Unificationists are seriously engaged in their International One World Crusade (IOWC) all over the United States. Reverend Moon sees America as God's "Chosen People" with a special role in divine providence for worldwide social reform. Horowitz recognized this when he called it "a movement without boundaries, expressing belief systems at once political and theological, outlining premises for political action and religious alignment."[7] This ultimate commitment is reminiscent of Robert Bellah's earlier description of America's civil religion, a comparison that was noted and paraphrased in an excellent analysis by Thomas Robbins and colleagues. Concentration on the Moonies as a "world-transforming" social movement tends to shift attention from family and religion as the core of the Unification Church.[8] Nevertheless, the spiritual conversion that begins in the heart of each member extends to each one's marriage and family and then to the larger society. The Unification mandate is a reform movement reaching out into the public realm and it offsets the speculations of many sociologists who emphasize the "privatization" of both religion and family.

The interpretation of the Unification Church as a religious reform movement emphasizes an organization that is "in process," but it must also be interpreted from a structural perspective. In choosing to call his religious following an association, Reverend Moon was employing acceptable sociological terminology. Large American churches and denominations are properly described as voluntary associations,[9] and this seems to fit the large, extended religious "kinship" of the movement. In this broader scope of membership and organization the Unification Church is seen as a large "secondary" collectivity to distinguish it from local communities like the Barrytown seminary, the World Mission Center, fundraising teams, and local home churches, maintained as primary, face-to-face groups. Both as a social movement and as a religious association, the church is always an "interest group," organized for purposes beyond the satisfaction of its own membership.

Although properly conceptualized in sociological terms as both a movement and an association, this religious collectivity uses ecclesiastical terms in its claim to be a Christian church. When the Holy Spirit Association applied for membership in the National Council of Churches of Christ on September 4, 1975, it confidently identified itself as "a Christian church committed to the ministry of spreading by word and deed the Gospel of the Divine Lord and Savior, Jesus Christ." This petition for affiliation was denied after the doctrines and scriptures of the church had been scrutinized and declared "non-Christian" by a subcommittee of four theologians appointed by the National Council's Commission on Faith and Order.

The members of this investigating committee are almost apologetic in pointing out that there is "much diversity" in the teachings of various Christian churches as well as "internal disagreement" in any given church. Nevertheless, there is some "ecumenical convergence" concerning certain essential and indispensable characteristics of the Christian faith. While fully defending "the freedom of the Unification Church to exist and propagate its beliefs," the subcommittee is forced to "conclude that the Unification Church is not a Christian church because its doctrine on the nature of the triune God is erroneous; its Christology is incompatible with Christian teaching and belief; and its teaching on salvation and the means of grace is inadequate and faulty." Furthermore, the "revelations invoked as divine and normative in *Divine Principle* contradict the basic elements of Christian faith."[10]

The Unified Family

Finally, the members of the Unification Church like to be known also by their shorter title, the Unified Family, which appears to be more widely used in Great Britain than in the United States.[11] The whole church is perceived as a "true family" in which Reverend Moon and his wife are the "true parents" of the members, who are their spiritual children. This is not the same as a large ecclesiastical organization which is made up of families as its units of membership. One of the basic tenets of revealed scripture, *Divine Principle,* is the "four-position foundation," which is manifested as "God, husband

and wife, and their offspring." The essential point to comprehend here is that religion is the most important ingredient in marital and familial love. This is not quite the same as saying with William D'Antonio that "love is the most important ingredient in religion," although Unificationists are fully ready to agree.[12] These concepts require clarification as we proceed to analyze the familial-ecclesial relationships in the Holy Spirit Association.

Who are the members of this familial-ecclesial organization and where do they come from? Only now are children beginning to be born into the American church. In late 1983 the church monthly newspaper began to publish pictures of babies born to those couples who had been married at the 1982 mass wedding at Madison Square Garden. These belong to the first generation of "Moonie-born" native Americans. In any large gathering of Moonies there is likely to be a significant proportion of Orientals, mainly Korean and Japanese who came to this country as missionaries. Among the non-Orientals in the American membership, there is no distinct ethnic proportion: their names are French, German, Hispanic, Irish, Italian, Polish or just typically "American." There is more than a "token" number of blacks in the family of God. This interracial and interethnic mixture is deliberately fostered in the church because the unification of world Christianity is intended to bring together believers from all races and nations.

Even with this international composition of the membership, the Unification Church in America tends to reflect Oriental characteristics. Many of the members are studying the history and language of Reverend Moon's native country and are developing a taste for Korean cuisine. Other immigrant religions, like German Lutheranism and Irish Catholicism, became Americanized over a generation or two. In some degree the reverse process seems to occur in the Koreanization of the American Moonies. As Christians speak reverently of Bethlehem and Nazareth, the Unificationists know from the revelation of *Divine Principle* that Korea is God's "chosen" nation as the birthplace of their prophet and leader.[13]

It is the American-born Moonies who now do most of the domestic missionary activity, and the church continues to grow both by birth and by conversions. Demographic statistics have not been carefully gathered and the available figures tend to shift. One interesting source of background information about the members—although restricted only to the individual informants—is the series of conferences in which participants related their own religious experience and conversion.[14] One young lady said she had been Episcopalean, but "went to many different churches and different Christian groups." Another said she "grew up in a very conservative Mennonite home." One former Catholic said she "went to mass and communion every day for one year and thought seriously about religious community." Another ex-Catholic, a male, reported that he "attended Catholic grammar school, high school, and university." A young man said, "I am a Jew from a middle-class home, and my mother was a militant atheist." A woman remarked, "I was born and raised in Israel in a kibbutz.' One Mexican-American female said, "I was raised in a Roman Catholic family, but we were also shamanistic."

In the early years of my acquaintance with the Unification Church I was puzzled by the number of former Roman Catholics who seemed to think that they could be both Catholic and Moonie. They maintained a deep and personal devotion to Reverend Moon and proclaimed loyalty to the Unification Church, its doctrines and practices. It is not unusual to hear a member say that since the Unification Church embraces all peoples in all religions "you don't have to give up your own church when you join." One former Lutheran likes to attend the Lutheran religious services whenever he has the opportunity. One young woman said that her parents want her to be married in the Catholic Church and asked whether I could arrange a nuptial mass for her and her intended spouse after the Moonie wedding ceremony.

In some instances, however, these young people were disillusioned with their previous church, even while they maintained a strong belief in God. In general they did not come from a position of religious ignorance; most of them had been reading about religion and searching for an acceptable church affiliation. Nor did they come from disadvantaged or broken homes. Eileen Barker, who has studied Moonies both in Britain and the United States, found that their new religion "is not in compensation for material deprivation but rather is an *escape* from materialism."[15] The young Moonie converts are in their early and mid-twenties when they join the church, have had more than average years of schooling, and have not suffered the psychic, social or economic deprivations that are said to drive some people to "deviant" religious sects.

Since the Unification Church is reputedly a "caring" community in which a familial spirit of love is expressed among the members, the assumption is sometimes made that young people flee to it as a refuge from unloving homes, hateful parents, and families rife with hostility. As a matter of fact, most of them report that their family of origin is friendly, with fairly pleasant relations between parents and children and among the siblings. Obviously, the fully committed Moonies leave their homes and dedicate themselves to the service of the church. In most instances they maintain good relations with their parents. "The hypothesis that people become Moonies because they are seeking the family atmosphere they never had does not fit the facts nearly so well as the hypothesis that they wish to continue or repeat the experience of a close and loving family."[16] Even those families that feel a "sense of outrage" against the Moonies and want to kidnap their children seem to be demonstrating particular parental love for them.

The Familial-Ecclesial Thesis

The religious beliefs and practices of the Unification Church are deliberately centered on family roles and relations. We have noted that this is an active religious movement that cannot be contained in the designation of either cult or sect. Although the Moonies were refused corporate affiliation with the National Council of Churches on the basis that their theology is non-Christian, there can be no doubt that they constitute a religion and a church in terms of Durkheim's accepted definition of "a unified system of beliefs and practices relative to sacred things, that is to say, things set apart and forbidden—beliefs and practices which unite into one single moral community called a church, all those who adhere to them."[17] Among the "sacred things" of the church are the promotion of marital fidelity and family solidarity as the basis of ecclesial unity.

The church of Reverend Moon is still in its infancy, with aspirations to become a universal religion which "desires to cover the whole life of humanity." It is already well organized and tends to approach the "ideal" church-type envisioned by Max Weber and elaborated by Ernst Troeltsch. It is overwhelmingly conservative and reaches out to the masses. Apparently, the Unification Church aims to utilize the state and the ruling classes and to weave these elements into her own life. As Troeltsch remarks, "She then becomes an integral part of the existing social order; from this standpoint, then, the church both stabilizes and determines the social order."[18] Students of sociology will recognize this description of the universal *ecclesia* which is said to have been approximated by medieval Catholicism. This is no less than the Moonie ambition to unify world Christianity.

It is true that the Moonies do not have a sacramentally ordained clergy, but they are led by a ministry of full-time functionaries. They are inspired by the divine revelation of the Old and New Testaments, but their central scripture is the volume called *Divine Principle*. Besides a full-time ministry and a holy book, the Unification Church possesses the four elements that sociologists find essential to every organized religion: the theological creed, the code of moral behavior, the system of worship services, and the structure of social relations.

Do we have here a church that acts like a family or a family that acts like a church? Sommerfeld speculates that the familial-type church can be distinguished from the democratic and the dominical types because it "views the Ultimate primarily in terms of divine family relationships."[19] In the Orthodox Christian tradition this means that the three persons of the Divine Trinity are emphasized less for their "roles" as Father, Son and Holy Spirit than for their relations as a "family." It seems unlikely that this theological conception accounts for the social organization of any church along the lines of familial relations. If this were the case, then all Christian churches that accept the doctrine of the Trinity should be identified as familial types. In western experience, however, the title "Holy Family," when applied to a local parish church, is in honor of the family of Mary, Joseph and Jesus.

The Lord's prayer, "Our Father," is probably the most frequently recited of all prayers among Christians everywhere who praise the divine Father and his blessings. Believers pray to the Son and the Holy Spirit, asking them to intercede with the Father as an analogy to earthly human relations, where petitions are ultimately addressed to the head of the family. It is purely imaginative, however, to speculate that a patriarchal church, as well as a patriarchal society, evolves from the creedal affirmation of God the Father.[20] It is an interesting fact, however, that no local parish church is named after the divine Father, while many carry the title of the Holy Spirit or of Christ. In the encyclical *Divinum Illud Munus,* we are reminded that "we should adore one God in Trinity and Trinity in Unity." The Pope relied on tradition when he said that "Our predecessor, Innocent XII, absolutely refused the petition of those who desired a special festival in honor of God the Father."[21]

While there is no evidence to support the hypothesis that all trinitarian belief systems lead to a familial-type religious organization, or that all people who worship God the Father build a patriarchal kind of church, the fact is that the Unification Church deliberately models itself on a family system and focuses its worship on God, the Father of all creation. Jesus is not God, but is a "true" spiritual Father. The Holy Spirit is not God, but is a "true" spiritual mother. The love between these two infuses a new life, a "spiritual rebirth" for the believer in Christ.[22] All the Moonie members are caught up in a religious family solidarity, although they were physically born into different racial, ethnic and religious backgrounds.

While we are focusing here on family concepts applied to the religious structures of the Moonies we must ever be aware of religious concepts applied to their family life. Sociologists have found the so-called "nuclear family" universal in human society with the basic functions of reproduction, sexual relations, economic cooperation, and socialization of offspring. The Unificationists are not only promoting the development of the "extended family" but are also insisting that religion must be an essential function of the family. Whatever else may characterize the familism of Reverend Moon's followers the religious role in family life remains of central importance.

Familistic Relations

The Unificationist dream that a religious collectivity can function as a large happy family is not a new one. The autonomous Benedictine abbey is a celibate brotherhood that maintains a kind of family spirit as long as its members remain relatively few. A typical contemporary example is the Charismatic Renewal Movement, which tried to remain spontaneous, informal and unstructured, but inevitably succumbed to routinization and institutionalization.[23] The evolution of the religious body from the small sect to a large *ecclesia* has been frequently described by sociologists who recognize that the initial family model ultimately expands into the model of bureaucracy.[24]

Like other small religious groups with aspirations for intimate personal relationships based on family patterns, the Unification Church has had to respond to the demands of expansion. Sorokin described the evolution from familistic relations in the small community to contractual relations in the large association, and indicated that even relations within the family—husband and wife, parents and children —were becoming contractual.[25] Reverend Moon believes that it is possible under religious inspiration to offset this development by insisting on a familial social structure for the church. This ideal is inculcated in the membership, as expressed by one American member: "I believe that he is my spiritual father. He is trying to bless us and bring us into perfection as individuals and as families. The idea of True Parents is a necessary symbol to bring mankind to the consciousness of being one family."[26]

At the lower echelons of the church the members are siblings by spiritual adoption, sisters and brothers who are spiritual children of their "Father in the Faith," as the Catholic seminarian may think of his bishop as his spiritual father, or as the Catholic laity everywhere look with filial devotion to the Holy Father in the Vatican. The spiritual childhood of Moonies is a temporary status that changes with the passage of years. Practically all of the young Americans who are attracted to the Unification Church are unmarried, and their status of spiritual childhood endures while they are being socialized into the Unified Family. The concept of the church as a kinship group, and the vision of the total world society as an enormous extended family, must necessarily have places for the elderly as well as the young, for the poor as well as the middle class and wealthy.

People grow away from their families of origin and sometimes also leave their churches, but they cannot completely opt out of society. It seems quite clear that Reverend Moon's background was influenced by the fact that "the Confucian society regards itself as a large family."[27] He seems intent on binding family, church and society in an unbreakable web of personal relationships. Confucian philosophy blends with Unification ecclesiology. The pivotal role of the family is not only a source of socialization for young people, and the virtues are respect, generosity and compassion; it is also the continuing model of altruistic social relations in the large community. "It personalizes and deepens the ties which bind men together to advance the common good. Thus, filial piety undergirds a stable, just and peaceful social order."[28]

Creeping Bureaucracy

The filial piety of the spiritual child in the Moonie family translates to the humble obedience of the newest recruits to the church. From the perspective of social status, the hardworking fundraisers are mainly in the lower ranks, doing what is often considered disagreeable tasks. Motivation for soliciting money and for persuading newcomers to visit the local center is seen also as fulfilling the condition of "indemnity," a form of penitential restitution to God for the sins of the world. "Life is organized around the center leader, whose closest counterpart is the abbot of a monastic community now made coed."[29] When a group is "on the road" together the mission leader often becomes the model or "the significant other" for younger members. Gradually with experience the evangelistic tasks meld into philanthropic tasks as the younger people become veteran members and then assume more responsibility as "central figures." Promotions are not accompanied by increased income. As a matter of principle there are no salaried members at any level of the church organization, and everybody lives and works under a missionary system.[30]

One need not be a prophet to suggest that while familistic relations may continue among small primary face-to-face groups in the church and at the local level of the Home Church that limits itself to 360 households in the immediate neighborhood, the larger and more complex the Unification Church becomes the more it will develop contractual relations in a bureaucratic organization. Sontag also makes this prediction: "I see the movement inevitably evolving into another established church, and I am not sure that this can be prevented, although constant reform and renewal can keep the original spirit alive."[31] If the church does not evolve into a bureaucratic structure, it is most likely to collapse. Indeed, realistic evidence on this point is provided by Harrison's study of the American Baptist Convention, which sees itself as an informal congenial fellowship. Harrison concludes that if the convention had not built a bureaucratic structure, "the result would have been no effective leadership, complete separation of the local congregations, an absence of common symbols, limited interchurch communication, no denominational unity, and no evangelical program."[32]

Whatever else may be said about the paternalistic and patriarchal polity of the Unification Church at the higher administrative levels, the brothers and sisters who live in communal centers and who work together on team tasks continue to demonstrate primary, personal and familistic relations. Growing experience in the Home Church Movement is extending this loving relation of service to non-Moonie strangers. Interviews with the Moonies and casual observation of their expressions of group solidarity indicate that they put higher value on human relations than on social structures. They seem determined to focus on family life in the Home Church rather than on a parochial house of worship.

Gazing into the future, Reverend Moon says: "Gradually we will be moving into family settlements. We will have our own enterprises and businesses. In the future we will have many, many places where families can be productive, raise their children, and build schools to educate their children." He has no intention to organize parishes, dioceses, judicatories, or vicariates. "I emphasize that our movement has always been centered about families as the basic unit of the heavenly society. The family emphasis is always the same. This means that more blessings in marriage will be given, more children will be born, more families will be created. Then we will become elevated from the personal communal type of centers to family-oriented homes. The family will always be the basic unit of happiness and cornerstone of the Kingdom of God on earth and thereafter in Heaven."[33]

Footnotes

1 Young Oon Kim, *Unification Theology,* New York, Holy Spirit Association, 1980, pp. 19-23. See also Neil Salonen, "History of the Unification Church," pp. 163-183, in Richard Quebedeaux, ed., *Lifestyle,* New York, Rose of Sharon Press, 1982

2 Warren Lewis, "Is the Reverend Sun Myung Moon a Heretic?" pp. 167-219, in M. Darrol Bryant and Herbert Richardson, eds., *A Time for Consideration,* New York, Mellen Press, 1978

3 Frederick Sontag, *Sun Myung Moon and the Unification Church,* Nashville, Abingdon, 1977, pp. 102-105

4 Geoffrey Nelson, "The Concept of Cult," *Sociological Review,* vol. 15, November 1968, pp. 351-362. See also David Martin, "A Definition of Cult: Terms and Approaches," pp. 27-42, in Joseph Fichter, ed., *Alternatives to American Mainline Churches,* New York, Rose of Sharon Press, 1983

5 For references to Troeltsch and Becker, as well as the Charismatics, see Joseph Fichter, *The Catholic Cult of the Paraclete,* New York, Sheed and Ward, 1975, pp. 19-38

6 See Lewis M. Killian, "Social Movements: A Review of the Field," pp. 9-53, in Robert R. Evans, ed., *Social Movements,* Chicago, Rand McNally, 1973

7 Irving Horowitz, ed., *Science, Sin and Scholarship,* Cambridge, MIT Press, 1978, "Sun Myung Moon: Missionary to Western Civilization," pp. xiii-xviii

8 See Thomas Robbins *et al.,* "The Last Civil Religion: Reverend Moon and the Unification Church," *Sociological Analysis,* vol. 37, no. 2, 1976, pp. 111-125

9   For analysis of "Groups and Associations" see chapter 4 in Joseph H. Fichter, *Sociology*, University of Chicago Press, 1971

10 See "Critique of the Theology of the Unification Church, as Set Forth in *Divine Principle*," by Agnes Cunningham, J. Robert Nelson, William L. Hendricks, and Jorge Lara-Braud, in Horowitz, *op. cit.*, pp. 102-118

11 See Mark Cozin, "A Millenarian Movement in Korea and Great Britain," pp. 100-121, in Michael Hill, ed., *A Sociological Yearbook of Religion in Britain*, London, SCM Press, 1973

12 William V. D'Antonio, "The Family and Religion: Exploring a Changing Relationship," *Journal for the Scientific Study of Religion*, vol. 19, June 1980, pp. 89-104. Marital love is related to "variables such as income and education," and perhaps also religion

13 *Divine Principle*, "That Nation of the East Is Korea," pp. 520-532

14 Typical are the "theological conversations" held at Berkeley and reported by Darrol Bryant and Durwood Foster, eds., *Hermeneutics and Unification Theology*, New York, Rose of Sharon Press, 1980, pp. 1-43

15 Eileen Barker, "Free to Choose? Some Thoughts on the Unification Church and Other Religious Movements," *The Clergy Review*, vol. lxv, Part I, October 1980, pp. 365-368; Part II, November 1980, pp. 392-398

16 *Ibid.*, 396. See also Carroll Stoner and Jo Anne Parker, *All God's Children: The Cult Experience*, New York, Penguin Press, 1979, p. 216. Most parents "were honestly attempting to assess if what their children had found was salvation, as they claim, or slavery, as the cult critics claim, or something in between."

17 Emile Durkheim, *The Elementary Forms of the Religious Life*, New York, Free Press, 1965, p. 62

18 Ernst Troeltsch, *The Social Teaching of the Christian Churches*, New York, Harper, 1960, p. 331

19 Richard Sommerfeld, "Conceptions of the Ultimate and Social Organization of Religious Bodies," *Journal for the Scientific Study of Religion*, vol. 7, Fall 1968, pp. 178-196

20 The practice of patriarchy either in religion or society did not come out of a developed Christian theology, says Sidney Callahan, *The Illusion of Eve*, New York, Sheed and Ward, 1965, p. 92

21 Promulgated by Pope Leo XIII in 1897, it was later reprinted in an English translation as "Encyclical on the Holy Ghost," pp. 161-181, in *The Catholic Mind*, vol. 36, May 8, 1938

22 *Divine Principle*, p. 216

23 Joseph H. Fichter, *The Catholic Cult of the Paraclete*, New York, Sheed and Ward, 1975, pp. 145-148

24 See Earl D. Brewer, "Sect and Church in Methodism," *Social Forces*, vol. 30, 1952, pp. 400-408; also Bryan R. Wilson, "An Analysis of Sect Development," *American Sociological Review*, vol. 24, February 1959, pp. 3-15

25 See Pitirim Sorokin, *Society, Culture and Personality*, New York, Harper and Brothers, 1947, pp. 99-110, 457-466; also Joseph H. Fichter, *Sociology*, University of Chicago Press, 1971, chapter 5, "Communities"

26 As told to Sontag, *op. cit.*, p. 62

27 See Julia Ching, *Confucianism and Christianity*, New York, Harper and Row, 1977, p. 96

28   Young Oon Kim, *Unification Theology,* New York, Rose of Sharon Press, 1980, p. 78
29   Sontag, *op. cit.,* p. 163
30   Reported by Neil Salonen, "Overview of Unification Church Activities," pp. 281-304, in Darrol Bryant, ed., *Proceedings* of Virgin Islands Seminar, New York, Rose of Sharon Press, 1980
31   Sontag, *op. cit.,* p. 201
32   Paul Harrison, *Authority and Power in the Free Church Tradition,* Carbondale, Southern Illinois University Press, 1971, p. 78
33   Sontag, *op. cit.,* pp. 156-157

VI The Family of God

The popular slogan reminding us that "the family that prays together stays together" suggests that religious practices are a guarantee of family solidarity. Sociologists generally agree that basic cultural institutions tend to be functionally supportive of each other. The impact of religion on the family is recognized, "but it should not be forgotten that the influence is mutual. The family is an important buttress of the church, helping inculcate attitudes conducive to committed church membership and the support of religious principles, just as the church provides legitimation for dominant family values and practices."[1] The effectiveness of this mutual bond is now being questioned under the hypothesis of secularization that the "breakdown" of the modern family is a correlative of the weakening of religious faith and practice.

Although most textbooks in family sociology report that the church exercises certain "controls" over family behavior, they seldom suggest that religion is a family activity. Sociological research at an earlier time revealed that the family provided multiple activities: economic, educational, recreational, and religious. The research report on sociocultural trends, done by William Ogburn in the early 1930s, included a discussion of the religious functions of the American family.[2] The classic anthropological research reported later by George Murdock did not list religion among the universal and essential functions of the family.[3] It is an interesting fact, however, that sociologists of religion are less likely to discuss the function of religion in the family than are the family sociologists. These latter scholars seem much more interested in the way the church "controls" the family than in the way it provides "support" for family members.[4]

While the functions of religion and family tend in some respects to intermingle, these two basic institutions require separate analysis. It is obvious to the ordinary churchgoer that his home is a place quite distinct from his church, and that in most aspects his family operates quite independently of his church. Nevertheless, there are persistent traditions that these two institutions are in many ways inseparable, if not identical. Roberts has no hesitancy in asserting that "traditionally the black church has been an extended family and the family has been a 'domestic church.' At the center of this affirmation is the Biblical image of the church as the family of God." Even outside and beyond Christianity, "throughout the African/Afro-American tradition the family system has been central to understanding the church —its purpose and mission. At the same time religion has been the core of fulfilled family."[5]

Another clear example of the close ties between religion and family is found in the traditions of Judaism, where it is said that "the synagogue is, in a sense, merely the lengthened shadow" of the Jewish home and family. This means, of course, that significant religious practices occur in the midst of the family, especially the weekly observances on Friday night. Domestic virtues are religious virtues and their combination, in the view of one author, make "the Jewish home the most vital factor in the survival of Judaism and the preservation of the Jewish way of life, much more than the synagogue or school." Heinrich Heine, the German poet, suggested that the Jewish home is a kind of "portable religion," because wherever the Jewish family has wandered over the centuries the Jewish religion was kept alive.[6]

The most noted contemporary bonding of religion and family is demonstrated in the Holy Spirit Association for the Unification of World Christianity, which derives its religion from the Judeo-Christian tradition and its familism from the ancient Confucian system. The Unificationists never tire of proclaiming that their church is a "United Family." The devout brothers and sisters see themselves as members of the "True Family" in which Reverend Sun Myung Moon and his wife are the "True Parents." A basic tenet of their revealed scripture, *Divine Principle,* is the "four-position foundation," which is manifested as "God, husband and wife, and their offspring." The church has its foundations in Korea where the Confucian philosophy of the extended family continues in strong vogue. The Confucian philosophy blends with Unification ecclesiology with the intent to bind family, religion and society in an unbreakable web of personal relationships.

For these reasons, the Unification Church presents an opportunity to investigate the extent to which an organized church is also essentially familistic.[7] We shall here explore the basic teachings and practices of the Unificationists in the following categories: (a) the theological creed, (b) the code of moral behavior, (c) the system of worship services, and (d) the structure, or polity, of social relations. The conceptual framework of this analysis is obviously that of the sociology of religion rather than the sociology of the family because we are asking how familistic concepts are found among the beliefs and practices of the Unification religion. Nevertheless, contained within this analysis are the answers a family sociologist may seek to the question whether religiosity is found in Moonie marriage and family.

Familistic Theology

The nature of God and the doctrine of salvation are among the Moonie theological doctrines that are patently familistic. The Unificationist sees God as the Parent who gave life to all human beings and as the loving Father who actually suffers because his heart has been wounded by the sins of his children. The Almighty God is not only the creator and preserver of all human life, but also "Father of Heart, subject being of Limitless Love."[8] God has intended from all eternity that human beings should form an intimate relationship with the Creator, a relationship of father and child, of lover and beloved, and thus be a reflection of God's perfect image and likeness. This familial bond with God is taken quite literally and constitutes the perfection of individuality which is God's "first blessing" to man. *Divine Principle* reveals: "This means that man attains deity. Feeling exactly what God feels and knowing God's will, he would live as God would want."[9]

It is clear, therefore, that the God of the Moonies is not the timeless Absolute of the Greek philosophers, or the unmoved mover of the Scholastic metaphysicians. God is not aloof and unapproachable, an awesome monarch who must be constantly placated. The nature of God in the Unification belief system is similar to the interpretation of process philosophers like Alfred Whitehead, and of process theologians who say that "God is concerned with the world; he is involved in its suffering and its tragedy. The world, man, and human events make a difference to him."[10] The intimate and personal responsibility of the Unificationist is "to alleviate God's sorrow, restore his sovereignty, and fill his heart with happiness." The Moonies speak sympathetically of the "injured Heart of God—the suffering of the Heavenly Father," who feels "crushed by the betrayal of his trusted and beloved ones."[11]

The personal relationship between the human creature and the loving fatherly creator is the first stage in the Unification scheme of eternal salvation. This divine-human relationship must be multiplied in social, familistic relationships among the children of God. No person is meant to be single and celibate and separate from other persons. It is a basic tenet of *Divine Principle* that God works in history essentially through the God-centered family. It is the vocation of males and females to "seek togetherness," which involves not only personal fulfillment and the production of offspring but also the social progress of humanity toward the Kingdom of God. In other words, the salvation of society, as well as of individual persons, cannot be achieved unless it emerges from a family-centered foundation. In terms of Unification theology, "the family ties which bind together God, husband, wife and children prove the fundamental pattern for all worthwhile forms of human relatedness."[12]

The place and function of the family in the Moonie scheme of salvation cannot be understood apart from the original sin of Eve and Adam at the beginning of human history, and from the ultimate establishment of the Kingdom of God after the Second Coming. According to the theology of *Divine Principle*, God intended this first couple to marry and have perfect children who would populate his physical and spiritual kingdom on earth. These perfect children in the God-centered family fit a Confucian ideal which gives dignity to marriage and procreation because the child is born in collaboration of husband, wife *and heaven* so that "anyone may be called the son of his mother or the son of heaven."[13] The divine intention was frustrated when Eve was sexually seduced by the archangel Lucifer, causing the *spiritual* Fall of mankind. Her impurity was transmitted in premature and illicit intercourse with Adam, causing the *physical* Fall of mankind.

Before this unfortunate double sin the first parents were sinless, but they had not achieved the first blessing of individual perfection. "They were in the stage of communicating directly with God when they fell and caused their offspring to fall into ignorance of God."[14] They could not achieve the important second blessing, God-centered marriage, until the messiah could redeem humanity from its inherited sinfulness. Jesus came on earth, accomplished his spiritual mission, but was killed before he could marry and father a new race of perfect children. The establishment of God-centered families is then the essential link between the sinful past and the prophetic millenium. Without the second blessing of perfect parents who produce large numbers of perfect children, the human race cannot be in readiness for the Second Advent of the messiah.

Orthodox Christian doctrine includes a belief in the divinity of Christ and a belief that redemption for sinful creatures comes through his suffering and death. On the contrary, Reverend Moon said: "One of my most important revelations is that Jesus Christ did not come to die. He came to this world to consummate his messianic mission given by God, which is the establishment of the Kingdom of God here on earth. Through his Crucifixion, however, Jesus gave himself as a sacrifice for the faithlessness of the world, and by his Resurrection he established spiritual salvation."[15] The Moonies hold Jesus in great reverence, have a personal and prayerful relationship with him, but do not accept his divinity.[16] He was the Lord of the First Advent who was to provide both spiritual and physical redemption for the full restoration of the human race to God, the Father. It is the goal of faithful Unificationists to lay the foundation for the Second Advent through God-centered marriage and family.

The Moral Code

The second essential element in any organized religion is constituted by its system of morality, the code of behavior which the members of the church promise to observe. The Moonies, like others in the Judeo-Christian tradition, accept the behavioral norms as a generalization of the kinds of moral conduct that people in western culture should exhibit. It is by following the law of God that they do the will of the creator and father who loves them. This is the path of personal perfection that unites them with God. Nevertheless, they have inherited the "fallen nature" of man which derives from the evil characteristics transmitted from Lucifer to Eve and Adam and their descendants. Because of this original sin, we "find ourselves in a boundary situation between the happiness of paradise and the agony of hell. When we act morally we side with God and when we sin we cement our alliance with Satan."[17]

Satan is very real for the Unificationists, and so is sin, but they recognize their responsibility to avoid sin and practice virtue. The primordial transgression of the first parents is the root of all subsequent sinfulness, and any human being can commit "individual sin" by forming a "reciprocal base with Satan." This does not mean that human freedom and responsibility have been usurped by the dominance of Satan. Indeed, by contrast, the person who leads a virtuous life does so by forming a "reciprocal base with God" instead of with Satan. The power of the Devil, however, must be taken seriously because "the objects of Satan are the evil spirits in the spirit world."[18]

While the Unification code of conduct includes all the patterns of Judeo-Christian morality, both personal and social, the most serious prohibition is on the "eschatalogical final sin." The ancient Jewish world of the Old Testament recognized the nature of this sin and in later centuries "adultery in the Talmud is considered such a serious sin that it can only compare with idolatry and murder."[19] It is no wonder that the Unificationists deplore the contemporary relaxation of sexual mores in literature and entertainment, in private and public life, and especially in the breakdown of the family system. The *Divine Principle* sees its broader implications as "the principal cause of the downfall of numerous nations, national heroes and patriots." Other sins may be eradicated through religion, education and improved social conditions, but in the modern world the crime of adultery "has become increasingly prevalent as the development of civilization makes human life easier and more indolent."[20]

Turning from the proscription of vice to the prescription of virtue, the Unification moral code promotes the God-centered family as the source and model of all moral behavior. While the Confucian ideology of the Korean culture differs from the Christian culture of Western society, Reverend Moon's moral system reveals a syncretistic combination of Christianity and Confucianism with obvious "resemblances between Unification theology's family-centered ethic and Confucian morality."[21] Filial piety is the first of all Confucian virtues, and family relations provide the model for all other types of social behavior. As among the Confucians, the Unificationists insist on the intimate relationship between family and religion. "The family has always been the center of Confucian life and ethics, and family life itself has demonstrated the nature of Confucianism itself, not only as a system of ethics, but also as a philosophy of religion."[22]

The minimal and essential purpose of the family institution, as viewed by sociologists who tend to emphasize the so-called "nuclear" family, is to provide for the regulation of sexual relations and for the introduction of children into society and their education. It is probably correct to say that in all human societies "marriage defines a responsibilty of the partners in terms of sexual behavior, child-rearing, inheritance, and the provision of food and other necessities."[23] The Moonies are impatient with sociological talk of "open marriage" and "alternative lifestyles" and "creative divorce" in America just as they are hostile to the Communist system which destroys the extended family among the Chinese. The Unificationists are on the side of those experts who, as Lasch writes, "seek to rescue domesticity by reviving the extended family." They are unhappy about the "opposite solution, a further shrinkage of the family," and about the contemporary "renewed insistence that companionship, not child-rearing, is the essence of married life."[24]

The Unificationists not only favor the multiple functioning and intergenerational extended family but they think of their own religious fellowship itself as a large family. They see the "breakdown of the family" as a social and ethical calamity, an immoral handicap for both the society and the individual. There is, therefore, a logical relationship between the preservation of the total society, which depends upon the preservation of marriage, and the restoration of the family, which in turn depends upon the proper regulation of sexual conduct between the spouses. Adam and Eve failed their marriage because they were immature, and they failed also in constituting a God-centered family. As a result, all subsequent generations suffered. "Thus the restoration of marriage is understood by Reverend Moon to be the beginning of the restoration of mankind in the last days."[25]

The virtue of chastity is in practice a personal pattern of behavior, but because of its consequences for other human beings it must also be recognized as a social virtue. While the central concept of sexual morality is intimately aligned with behavioral patterns of relations between male and female, the Moonies recognize its broader and wider implications, and thus the full scope of morality. The principles of Unification moral conduct are based in the Judeo-Christian tradition of the Ten Commandments, and in the corporal and spiritual works of mercy as spelled out in the Beatitudes. Reverend Moon observed that "the degradation of the moral standards through drug problems, moral crises, and family problems is bringing American youth into a helpless position." In the larger view of society, he declared that he wanted to "revive the Christian spirit by igniting a new spiritual fervor with new spiritual truth."[26]

When the Unification Church is termed a "world-transforming movement,"[27] the connotation shifts it clearly beyond the question of personal purity and family spirituality. The ideology is geared to a complete moral reformation of all socio-cultural institutions: education, politics, economics, and recreation. The collective concern for the whole of society is demonstrated in the varieties of "social works" in which the church has been involved. Critics tend to focus on fund-raising techniques and refuse to believe that the funds are widely used in social services to the underprivileged. As Sontag remarks, "this church raises the issues of the deterioration of our family structure, the lethargy of many traditional religious institutions, the problem of religions intruding their goals into politics, and the religious control of money and power."[28]

Cultic Practices

The third basic dimension of every organized religion is that of shared ritual and public worship, patterns of piety and spirituality, which the members practice together to manifest their relationship with God. There is no sacramental or liturgical ceremony to symbolize initial public acceptance as a spiritual child of the Unified Family. The initiation to membership in the Unification family is relatively informal. The recruit simply begins to share in the common life of work and prayer. One of the more regular devotional patterns among the Moonies is Bible study and the discussion of scriptural texts. Most of them had some previous instruction in the Bible, both Old and New Testaments, which they now view as "an imperfect record written down by people, many of whom didn't understand what God was trying to say."[29] By divine inspiration and revelation their revered Father Founder produced *Divine Principle* as a clarification of what God really wanted to say through the message of holy scripture.

The most solemn repetitive ritual among the Unificationists is the Pledge, a prayer recited in unison at five o'clock in the morning on every Sunday, as well as on the first day of each month, and on the four annual holy days. The familistic significance of these holy days reflects the fact that the annual Parents' Day commemorates the wedding of Moon and his wife in Korea in 1960. Children's Day annually celebrates the birth of the Moons' first child the following year. The Pledge is recited on two other yearly festivals, the Day of

All Things and God's Day. The collective affirmation of the Pledge strengthens their determination as children of God to make any sacrifices required by the divine will, "to sow sweat for earth and tears for mankind." The brothers and sisters sit separately on different sides of the room, begin with three full bows to the floor as a sign of humility and respect to God. "Pledge is a time of rededication to God and to our mission as we remind ourselves why we joined the church and what we hope to accomplish."[30]

The less formal worship services are held twice a day wherever a group is living in community or in close proximity. Leadership of the service rotates among all the center members and includes song, scripture reading, prayer, and an interpretive message. The evening service consists of song and prayer, but includes, and is followed by, spiritual conversation and religious sharing. Sunday services are more formal and are open to the public. Berkeley Rice describes a Sunrise Service at the Belvedere Estate in Tarrytown, attended by about 500 members who had come up from New York City. They listened, "seemingly captivated," to Reverend Moon's sermon. After the sermon "an associate led the audience in a fifteen-minute prayer in which he asked repeatedly if they were willing to sacrifice themselves for the church."[31] With the rising sun they sang a church hymn, after which Reverend Moon concluded the worship service with a ten-minute prayer in the Korean language.

Evangelization and recruitment are essential spiritual tasks in which all members participate, individually and collectively. They are constantly seeking "spiritual children," newcomers who are welcomed joyously to affiliation with the Unified Family. The enactment of the spiritualized parent role is seen as practical experience in socializing converts and raising them in spiritual kinship. An added incentive is that they must have recruited three spiritual children before becoming eligible for matching and marriage. Introducing new members is also a preliminary learning process in preparation for the physical and spiritual parental role with their own natural children after marriage.

New Moonies do not just take out membership in a church; they become spiritual children of their recruiter into the Unified Family.

The disordering of family relations came about through the infidelity of Adam and Eve. The rebirth of fidelity to God comes through intimate affiliation with the restored Unified Family. Warren Lewis explains that "this spiritual-social family is seeking to be that group of people whose relationships are being perfected. Consistent with this view the sacramental life of Unification Church members is focused entirely upon the process of unifying with the family of the Lord of the Second Advent."[32] In dealing with prospective spiritual children the typical Moonie does not ask the fundamentalist question "Are you saved?" because conversation and salvation are seen as a process rather than an event.

There is no formal baptismal ceremony to symbolize entrance into the Unified Family. The usual pattern has been to invite the recruit to live in the local center until a personal decision has been made to affiliate, but even then the neophyte is not "fully" a member until married. Every Moonie has the "marital vocation" and is intended by God and by destiny for marriage and parenthood. The period of waiting for this real and special blessing is like a seminary training during which the many spiritual and material tasks of the ongoing church have to be performed. Living like the Moonies and with them, achieving a personal salvific relationship with God, and the maintenance of a celibate style of life are all preliminary to the well-documented "matching" of prospective spouses.

The prayerful preparation for this solemn and exciting ceremony precludes teenage marriages, or interfaith marriage with non-Moonies, or any other rash and thoughtless spouse selection. The formal ritualistic matching is unquestionably the deepest spiritual experience in the church life of the Moonie. From both a personal and ceremonial perspective this is the central happening of the Unificationist liturgy. It requires and reflects an enormous act of faith in the charismatic validity of Reverend Moon and a genuine personal trust that this commitment is indeed the mandate of Divine Providence. One member of Catholic background remarked that "just as you have faith in the miracle of the mass, we are ready to believe in the miracle of the matching." They have been in long prayerful preparation for this occasion; they know the pious quality of their spiritual siblings; they are not likely to be "taken by surprise," and they are usually quite ready to give mutual assent.

The religious ceremony that publicly recognizes this "engagement" is more than a simple declaration of intent to marry. It is a solemn binding betrothal, a "mandate from heaven" establishing a bond that is not to be broken under any condition. The exchange of the cup of "holy wine" is the marriage contract and symbolizes purification from sin of both spouses. Almost as an afterthought they have a civil and "legal" marriage, but "for Unificationists, the traditional sacraments of baptism, eucharist and holy matrimony happen all at once, one time only, on the glorious occasion of their 'blessing,' when they are married within their church and thereby are united permanently with their new family."[34] Since the founder of church is accepted as the "true parent" of both spouses he is modifying the Oriental Confucian-matching procedure by enacting a kind of "double paternity." Under the ancient rules of family discipline the father of the young man makes arrangements with the father of the prospective bride. This parental guidance in the choice of a mate is quite different from that of the traditional professional matchmaker, an "outsider" who is paid a fee.

The matched couple is already truly married but they do not live together even after the public liturgy of the subsequent spectacular mass wedding ceremony which is conducted from time to time by the "true parents," Reverend and Mrs. Sun Myung Moon. Multiple weddings were inaugurated in 1961 for the 36 blessed couples who still form the main Advisory Council for the church. The numbers increased to 72 couples in 1962, 430 couples in 1967, 777 couples in 1970 (when the first American members were included), 1,800 in 1975. The spectacular, and largest, wedding ceremony of 2,045 couples at Madison Square Garden in July 1982 was followed by a smaller mass wedding in Seoul the subsequent November. "The most prevalent feeling" among the spouses "was that God had been arranging the whole thing all along, that their mates had been created just for them. Master, knowing God's heart and will for each of them, had brought them together."[35]

The important symbolism of large multiple wedding ceremonies reflects the conviction that a marriage must be much more than a private contract between two people. The mass wedding demonstrates to the world that these couples are part of a large religious family, a Unified Church of all Christians under the fatherhood of God. This is a central doctrine of Unification thought and lifestyle. "The Blessing is a passport to heaven. Marriage has that purpose and significance. It is conceived in relationship to God. The blessing ceremony has sacramental qualities. It has elements of the traditional Christian sacraments, as well as much that is new and different. For example, during the wedding ceremony, holy water is used in a baptismal fashion and holy wine in a eucharistic manner. During the time of the Blessing ceremony, according to Unification theology, one's sins are forgiven and new life is given."[36]

Structure and Polity

The fourth essential element of an authentic organized religion is its group formation, the permanent association of members under some kind of polity. In ecclesiatical language, polity ranges from a loosely organized congregational system, with emphasis on the autonomy of lower-echelon members, to a tightly structured episcopal system, with functional control residing in the top leadership. The frequently stated ideal among the Unificationists is that of familistic relations within an extended kinship system. In actual practice, however, the Unification Church is a bureaucratic hierarchy, with authority emanating from the top leadership in the person of God's messenger and prophet. The well-known "five relationships" of Confucius, which are applicable to the extended Oriental family, have been modified by the Unificationists in their familial-ecclesial structure. One may properly say that "the relationships continue to require reciprocal duties and responsibilities, but the superior partners have more rights, and the inferior more duties."[37]

From the perspective of organizational polity, the church could best be called a paternalistic episcopal system with the benign ruler occupying the seat of authority by "divine right." The earthly head of the church is obviously Reverend Moon, who acts in the capacity of vicar for God, the Father of all humanity, while preparing for the Second Advent of the Messiah. He and Mrs. Moon are the "true parents" representing the third chance that God has provided for the restoration of the world. Adam and Eve failed. Jesus, the second Adam, had no Eve. The third Adam and (the second) Eve are the Moon couple. This is not the role of Messiah (although some fervent Moonies insist that it is) but that of a precursor to the Lord of the Second Coming. "I had to start with the role of John the Baptist in order to lay the initial foundation upon which I could construct my own mission." Reverend Moon states clearly that "the work of the Unification Church and my mission is to proclaim the coming of the messianic age."[38]

Reverend Moon is not an ordained, or enthroned, or crowned and mitred head of the church, but he is the acknowledged earthly leader to whom his followers bow as to their true paternal and spiritual mentor. There are no ordinary clergy in this church, no monsignors, archbishops, or eparchs. There is no sacred congregation of cardinals, but the revered patriarch is assisted in his fatherly governance by the members of the 36 blessed families, who trace back to the first mass public wedding in 1961 and who "represent the immediate personal foundation for the mission of Reverend Moon." His paternity depends also on the advice of informal counselors and he has chosen a president for the church in America, Dr. Mose Durst, who had previously been director of the church in northern California. The most recent reorganization of the American church has been into ten regions, each under the leadership of a veteran Korean Moonie.

At the intermediary level of the structure the Unification Church relies on so-called "central figures" characterized as territorial leaders in each state and in each local community center, or as functional leaders in the many enterprises in which members are engaged. While many women members have done excellent missionary work and have exhibited fine leadership qualities, the more important posts at the state and local levels are generally under the charge of male leaders. Feminists are likely to attribute the gender inequality among the Unification leadership to the patriarchal and Confucian philosophy of this ecclesial family. The ancient Korean kinship system had the female always subject to the male, the maiden to her father and elder brother, the wife to her husband, the widow to her son. It should be noted, however, that the first Moonie missionary to America, the main theologian of the church, is a woman, as is the academic dean of the Unification theological seminary at Barrytown.

At the lower echelons of the structure, the members are siblings by spiritual adoption, sisters and brothers who are spiritual children of their "Father in the Faith," as the Catholic seminarian may think of the bishop as his spiritual father, or as the Catholic laity everywhere look with filial devotion to the Holy Father in the Vatican. The spiritual childhood of the Moonies is a temporary status that changes with experience and the passage of years. Practically all of the young Americans who are attracted to the Unification Church are unmarried, and their status of spiritual childhood endures while they are being socialized into the Unified Family.

Aside from the category of full-time committed Unificationists there are older members who settle down to their roles in family, occupation and community while fostering activity in the "Home Church." There are also converts among the ordinary "laity" who accept the theological and moral doctrines of *Divine Principle* but have no intention of living in church centers. The concept of the church as a kinship group, and the vision of the total world society as an enormous extended family, must necessarily have place for the elderly as well as the young, for the poor as well as the middle class and wealthy. The development of the Home Church Movement, which was instituted by Reverend Moon in the summer of 1978, promises to engage the energy of the lay people who may do volunteer personal service to 360 households in the immediate neighborhood. It is also at this grass-roots level of membership that room can be made for widowed and divorced, for bachelors and single women who had not been caught up in the blessed vocation to marriage and family.

Footnotes

1 John Wilson, *Religion in American Society: The Effective Presence,* Englewood Cliffs, Prentice-Hall, 1978, pp. 238f
2 William F. Ogburn, "The Family and Its Functions," in *Recent Social Trends in the United States,* New York, McGraw-Hill, 1934
3 George P. Murdock, *Social Structure,* New York, Macmillan, 1949
4 See William V. D'Antonio, William M. Newman, Stuart A. Wright, "Religion and Family Life: How Social Scientists View the Relationship," *Journal for the Scientific Study of Religion,* September 1982, vol. 21, no. 3, pp. 218-225
5 J. Deotis Roberts, *Roots of a Black Future: Family and Church,* Philadelphia, Westminster, 1980, pp. 80, 86
6 See Arnold Dashefsky and Irving M. Levine, "The Jewish Family: Continuity and Change," pp. 163-190, in William V. D'Antonio and Joan Aldous, eds., *Families and Religions,* Beverly Hills, Sage, 1983
7 Frank K. Flinn notes, however, that two prominent Protestant theologians, Karl Barth and Paul Tillich, "hardly mention" marriage and family in their major treatises. See "Marriage as Eschatological Type," pp. 235-253, in Gene G. James, ed., *The Family and the Unification Church,* New York, Rose of Sharon, 1983
8 Young Oon Kim, *Unification Theology and Christian Thought,* New York, Golden Gate, 1976, revised edition, p. 38
9 *Divine Principle,* p. 43
10 See Alfred North Whitehead, *Process and Reality: An Essay in Cosmology,* New York, Macmillan, 1929, pp. 519-533, reprinted as "God and the World," pp. 85-99, in Ewert Cousins, ed., *Process Theology,* New York, Newman Press, 1971
11 Young Oon Kim, *op. cit.,* p. 40. The Catholic is reminded here of the once-popular devotion to the Sacred Heart of Jesus, which suffers because of sinful human behavior
12 Young Oon Kim, *Unification Theology,* New York, Holy Spirit Association, 1980, p. 76
13 Miles M. Dawson, *The Basic Teachings of Confucius,* New York, Home Library, 1915, p. 145
14 *Divine Principle,* p. 120
15 As told to Frederick Sontag, *Sun Myung Moon and the Unification Church,* Nashville, Abingdon, 1977, p. 134
16 See *Divine Principle,* pp. 342-371, "The Providence of Restoration Centering on Jesus." The question: "Is Jesus God Himself?" is answered in the negative, *ibid.,* p. 210
17 Young Oon Kim, *Unification Theology,* p. 229
18 For the connections among these various concepts see *Divine Principle,* pp. 83-95
19 Young Oon Kim, *Unification Theology and Christian Thought,* p. 49
20 *Divine Principle,* p. 75
21 Young Oon Kim, *Unification Theology,* p. 77
22 Julia Ching, *Confucianism and Christianity,* New York, Harper and Row, 1977, p. 97

23 Melvin DeFleur *et al., Sociology: Human Society,* Glenview, Scott Foresman, 1981, third edition, p. 443. See also their discussion of "The Family in Contemporary China," pp. 422-425

24 Christopher Lasch, *Haven in a Heartless World: The Family Besieged,* New York, Basic Books, 1977, p. 137

25 Frank K. Flinn, "Christian Hermeneutics and Unification Theology," pp. 141-166, in Darrol Bryant and Herbert Richardson, eds., *A Time for Consideration,* New York, Mellen Press, 1978

26 Frederick Sontag, *op. cit.,* pp. 156-157

27 Anson Shupe and David Bromley, "Characteristics of World-Transforming Movements," *Sociological Analysis,* vol. 40, no. 4, Winter 1979, pp. 326-328

28 Sontag, *op. cit.,* p. 21

29 Jonathan Wells, p. 56, in Darrol Bryant and Durwood Foster, eds., *Hermeneutics and Unification Theology,* New York, Rose of Sharon Press, 1980

30 Patricia Zulkosky, "Piety and Spirituality," pp. 51-71, in Richard Quebedeaux, ed., *Lifestyle,* New York, Rose of Sharon Press, 1982

31 Berkeley Rice, "The Pull of Sun Moon," pp. 226-241, in Irving Horowitz, ed., *Science, Sin and Scholarship,* Cambridge, MIT Press, 1978

32 Warren Lewis, "Is the Reverend Sun Myung Moon a Heretic?" pp. 167-219, in Darrol Bryant and Herbert Richardson, eds., *A Time for Consideration,* New York, Mellen, 1978

33 The matching ceremony is described by Hugh and Nora Spurgin, "Engagement, Marriage and Children," pp. 1-8, in Richard Quebedeaux, ed., *Lifestyle,* New York, Rose of Sharon Press, 1982

34 Warren Lewis, *op. cit.,* p. 190

35 Sontag, *op. cit.,* p. 167, together with photos of participants in the 1975 wedding ceremony in Seoul

36 Hugh and Nora Spurgin, *op. cit.,* p. 5

37 Ching, *op. cit.,* p. 99

38 As told to Sontag, *op. cit.,* pp. 131, 134

VII Home Church: Alternative Parish

Although the Unification Church is a relatively new organized religion, having been founded as recently as 1954 in Korea, it has become an alternative option for the growing number of young Americans who select it in preference to the church or denomination with which they had previously been affiliated. It was formally pronounced an alternative to Christianity when it was denied membership in the National Council of Churches of Christ. Its "heretical" doctrines were declared faulty, erroneous, inadequate and "incompatible with Christian teaching and belief."[1] Under this protocol, the Holy Spirit Association is said to differ theologically from the mainline American Protestant churches. There are many ways in which the Unification Movement is also culturally and sociologically different from most organized religious bodies, but at this point we discuss a unique structural element.

On the other hand, the Holy Spirit Association is structurally similar to most other well-established and highly organized religious denominations. It has a chain of command and communication from the newest fledgling member to the topmost hierarch. It has its own "Vatican" in New York and ten regional "judicatories" each under the authority of a Korean "cardinal." Every state in the Union now has its state director and urban centers, with appointed leaders analogous to ecclesiastical dioceses with their appointed bishops. It is at the lowest level of the structure where the Moonies have introduced a system of "Home Churches" in place of the conventional parishes and congregations. The focus of our discussion is an examination of this basic social unit as a substitute for the typical "worshipping community" to which Christians generally have become accustomed.

111

From a functional perspective the institution of Home Church meant that the dedicated Moonie would do less "street witnessing" to young people and begin to do "home witnessing" to whole families. In explaining this new mission one of the activists said that "with the coming of Home Church, everything seemed to turn around and take a completely different focus. Instead of approaching people on the streets or on campus, we began to visit people in their homes. Reverend Moon has asked each member of the Unification Church to take an area of three hundred and sixty homes in which to witness, serve and love the people with all our heart, all our soul and all our strength."[2]

The Moonie Laity

While the Unification Church does not have an ordained clergy, it seems inappropriate to say that the full-time leaders and core members are simply lay people. The active members of the church are typically described as dedicated young people who accost strangers in airports, bus stations, and street corners, soliciting funds for their worthy causes, or inviting prospective converts to share a meal or to attend a lecture at their center. In a sense, these are the trained professionals of the movement, analogous to young Mormons on missionary duty or to Catholic religious sisters and brothers who do not aspire to the ordained ministry. They are the full-time disciples of Reverend Moon whose religious zeal sometimes frightens their parents and makes the clergy nervous. They exhibit a spiritual enthusiasm so alien to the worldly materialism of the American culture that they are often viewed with suspicion, not only by secularists but also by regular churchgoers.[3]

When they first join the church, the young Moonies perform the dual tasks of fund-raising and witnessing, but with enough experience they soon assume the direction of a small mobile fund-raising team traveling about the country. This activity was reorganized and formalized in early 1983 when Reverend Moon instituted the International One World Crusade (IOWC) on a three-year schedule of proselytizing throughout the country. Aside from this missionary experience, most of the Unificationists also bring a variety of talent to the movement, from mechanics to musicians. Among them are lawyers, accountants, nurses, social workers, physicians, and other skilled and trained persons. Many specialized tasks, typical of expanding organizations, have to be filled at the New York headquarters as well as in foreign countries. Some members are selected to attend the Unification Seminary at Barrytown, New York, and after two years of study are sent to pursue doctoral studies at one of the better universities.

None of these full-time members, whether beginners at fund-raising, center leaders or state directors, special functionaries, seminarians or graduate students, can be called "laity" as the term is commonly applied to ordinary members of typical church parishes. None of them, not even Reverend Moon or his top associates, is salaried, but all are financially dependent on the church. These are the "insiders," fully engaged in the maintenance and furtherance of the total movement and always conscious that they are "committed to the ministry of spreading, by word and deed, the gospel of the Divine Lord and Saviour, Jesus Christ."

In any expanding religious movement or organization there has to be room for increasing numbers of lay associates who are not caught up in its full-time operation. These "lay" persons are of two kinds. There are now large numbers of Moonies who had been full-time functionaries of the church but are now married, settled down and with an occupation outside the church. One of these "veterans" said that he and his wife have contact with the center leader three or four times a week, give volunteer assistance to the group, and tithe regularly. "People come to a point in their lifetimes when they just don't see a way for themselves within the church structure. I think it's important for the church to be able to embrace these people, even if they no longer remain full-time church members."

There is another category of members who were never full-time, who have jobs and families and social ties which they intend to maintain even after conversion to the Unification Church. These seem to be the ordinary laity, who in other churches are the "modal" parishioners and are called "associates" by some center leaders.[4] Eileen Barker describes them as "people who accept, or at least feel a fairly strong sympathy for, the teachings presented in *Divine Principle* but who, for various reasons, do not commit themselves to living in a center or to working full-time for the UC."[5]

Except for the fact that they share the same adherence to the tenets of the Unification Church, these lay associates differ widely from the full-time Moonies. Males outnumber females by about two to one among the fully dedicated members, but this sex ratio is reversed among the lay associates. There is also an age difference, with the majority (80%) of the laity being over thirty years of age, while the same proportion of full-timers is under thirty. Perhaps mainly because of this age difference, the lay associates are less educated and with fewer years of college attendance, but are also more likely to be married.

The prospective convert who is a permanent spinster or bachelor promises to raise a doctrinal embarrassment for the church. The religious vocation of the full-fledged Moonie is a preparation for the blessed state of matrimony, with a Unificationist spouse chosen by Reverend Moon. This basic formula is important because the normal channel of salvation is the family lineage which brings redemption through blessed parents from generation to successive generations. This raises the question for prospective membership of persons who do not wish to be married, or who do not find the individual they would like to marry. At a Unification seminar the remark was made that the church's "theological emphasis is completely geared toward the notion of a heterosexual, monogamous marriage. With this as the center, other kinds of relationships do not seem possible or viable. Single people seem to be regarded somewhat like Cinderellas amidst the chosen people's family."[6]

It appears that as the number of lay converts increases and as the Home Church develops, room is being made among the associates for the "virgins and the bachelors." Mickler observes that "although the married state is perceived as normative, there exists a strong and significant tradition of single people in the life of the church."[7] Research data show about half of the laity are married, while three out of ten (28%) are separated, divorced or widowed, the remainder being single. This means that half of the lay associates are not now in the blessed state of marriage to which the fully committed members aspire or have already reached. This may be a partial reason why many give the impression that "they had been leading lonely and unsatisfied lives. One of their most frequent complaints was that the Unification Church did not use them enough. Their existence indicated that the Unification Church might appeal to a wider constituency than that from which the full-time Moonie was drawn, but that it succeeded in doing so only as long as it did not demand the kind of unquestioning devotion and sacrificial lifestyle that the young unmarried Moonie was prepared to give."[8]

The Flexible Non-Parish

The Home Church of which these lay Moonies are more the beneficiaries than the functionaries does not conform to the standard local parish. People who profess a religious faith and who live up to the rules of their faith tend to identify themselves as church members by affiliating with a local group of the same religious persuasion. From a theological perspective one may say that the central and identifying social function of the church congregation is the collective worship of God. Through song and ceremony, and through the preaching of the sacred scripture, the attention of the faithful is directed to the Lord. Christians come together on Sunday morning —perhaps after they have already heard their favorite televangelist— in order to give glory to God, to praise the Lord, to recite prayers of petition and thanksgiving. The traditional rituals of the Jewish temple or synagogue are centered on the deity. The buildings themselves, and the internal arrangement of furniture, tables and altars and pews, are at least symbolically pointed to God.

While it is often said that people do not need a church building in which to worship God, and that God "may be found" in the beauties of nature—in the mountains, at the seaside—there have always been *places* of worship. The shrines of antiquity, the temples of eastern religions and the cathedrals of western Christianity, attest to the historical tendency to settle on a specific location where groups of people can gather in common demonstration of their religious beliefs.[9] The place itself may become sacred as a magnet of pilgrims so that it no longer serves the particular local population for whom it was originally established. Similarly, the so-called "chapel of ease" attracts communicants in the downtown business and shopping districts where few parishioners actually reside. The noon mass on weekdays, novenas and other religious services, are provided for virtual transients.

These traditional parochial structures endured for centuries wherever Christians gathered in permanent residential areas, and they are still the predominant form of congregational organization.[10] Although their central function is to proclaim the religious relationship with God, there appear to be many instances in which a secondary function, that of "fellowship," takes precedence. The Protestant congregation is described by Gibson Winter as a center of attraction for people of similar social status among whom the preservation of an exclusive community is of some importance.[11] While typical urban Catholic parishes focused on spiritual and sacramental functions for all Catholics who lived in the parochial territory, regardless of their social status, they tended to neglect any deliberate attempt to develop solidarity, or a sense of parochial belongingness. They were seen as a kind of spiritual "service station" with a franchise from the bishop that required no effort to build community.

In the recent past, however, with the advent of "new" religions, the influence of charismatic and pentecostal programs, and the "quest" for community among young people, there have occurred certain modifications in the conventional local church, both the exclusive Protestant fellowship and the loosely structured Catholic parish. Some impetus was given by the Fathers of the Second Vatican Council for the renewal of both liturgy and community. "Efforts also must be made to encourage a sense of community within the parish, above all in the common celebration of the Sunday Mass."[12] The study of American communes and utopias shows that in many instances the solidarity of the members was strengthened by their deep commitment to religious values. In other words, the more successful communes, those that endured for the longest periods of time, were generally held together by shared religious beliefs and practices.[13] This is most obvious in centuries of experience in religious orders like the Benedictines, Carmelites and Franciscans.

While the basic organizational scheme tends to be similar in conventional Christian congregations, some variation is introduced according to size and type of population and location: Small rural churches differ from large urban and suburban congregations. The Protestant congregation differs from the Catholic parish in the degree of lay participation in decision-making and the sharing of religious functions, but in both instances the central figure is still the minister. Changes are occurring. The so-called "intentional" community and the "covenant" community are offered as a substitute for the traditional parish.[14] This is meant to strengthen solidaristic ties in small primary groups of the faithful and also to facilitate the fulfillment of religious obligations. The central goal is unity and solidarity, the building of community.

It should be pointed out that the purpose of the Unificationist Home Church is neither to provide a place of worship nor to build a local spiritual community. In keeping with their ultimate objective of unifying all religions as well as all people, the Moonies have no hesitancy in attending religious services in Christian churches, Jewish synagogues, Islamic mosques, or other houses of worship. There is an interesting parallel among the early disciples when Jesus was no longer among them. The *Acts of the Apostles* frequently recount that they "went up to the temple to pray," even though they participated also in the unique eucharistic meal, the chief act of collective worship, in the privacy of their own homes. Scripture scholars have called to our attention the role of "house churches" among the early Christians.[15] A more recent parallel developed when Chinese Christians were persecuted in the Cultural Revolution of the 1960s and their regular places of worship closed.[16] To substitute for the local church, they gathered in small numbers in many thousand "house churches," which soon came under the surveillance of the Peking government.

Origins of Home Church

The form and function of the Unificationist Home Church are not the same as those of the historical house church where Christians gathered for worship and prayer, nor of those in the typical urban Unification center which is used for much more than prayer services. The Home Church is not made up of the so-called "lay" people who are not in the full-time ministry of the church. We are left then with the concept that each individual Moonie, whether full-time or in associate status, is the foundation of the Home Church. If the Home Church is not a physical building or a gathered congregation, it must somehow encompass people to whom the individual Moonie will bring the church. Without knowing it, without signing up for membership, all of the residents in the nearest 360 household units are arbitrarily constituted a Home Church, regardless of their actual church affiliation, or lack thereof. All the residents of this designated neighborhood (which may be a college dormitory, a high-rise apartment building, or an institution) then become recipients of the Moonie ministry of service.

The flexibility of the Home Church program is demonstrated in its application by the Collegiate Association for the Research of Principles (CARP) which is the Unificationist form of campus ministry. Reverend Pak, the national director of CARP, explained that its Home Church area is the college campus community. "In other words, our home church area is the campus, the classroom, the plaza, the dorms, community centers, bookstores, hamburger stands. It is here that we must work to raise the spiritual consciousness of the community and find our spiritual children."[17] The core members also act as a catalyst by mobilizing an "associate membership" within the campus community.

This strategy of altruistic service is the main characteristic that sets the Unificationist Home Church apart from other local congregations and parishes. Although the use of the term Home Church became popular only in the summer of 1978 when Reverend Moon took the Barrytown seminarians to do missionary work in England and Scotland, the practice of altruistic service to strangers goes back to the pioneer days of the movement in Korea. It is a central theme of the Moonie theology of salvation that "we atone for our sins through specific acts of penance." The restoration of all things to the loving Father requires the believer to fulfill the "condition of indemnity."[18] Dedicating oneself to the service of others for a definite period of time is a means of atoning for the sins of humanity and satisfying the divine will.

It is a matter of record that Reverend Moon sent out his earliest converts on a forty-day pioneering mission; one of the first female followers was sent from Pusan to Taegu to work out this form of indemnity. This is still a practice among the Moonies and it is appreciated as an excellent preparation for the establishment of a home church. The trial period is reminiscent of the forty days during which the Hebrews doubted that Canaan was to be the Promised Land. Because of their lack of faith they were forced to wander in the desert forty years before God allowed them to enter Canaan. The individual Moonie sometimes says that these forty days of trial are an opportunity to "gain Canaan" for God as well as to gain the specific kinds of experience that helps in the successful operation of the Home Church.

A dedicated young German Moonie, who now has a responsible administrative position in the Unification Church, described this forty-day experience. For three days he attended a preparatory session in Frankfurt with fellow Moonies who had never had such experience. He left town with only twenty marks in his pocket and with no luggage, in order to be of service to the people in a rural community. "The first night I slept at the Red Cross, and the next two nights in a barn. One lady gave me fifty marks so I could find a place to sleep. That was enough to get a cheap hotel for three nights. I was selling the church magazine, *Neue Hoffnung,* but I really didn't need much money."

This young pioneer found that some people are distrustful and others have no need for volunteer services. He offered to help at two senior citizen homes and at the local Catholic parish, but these places had nothing for him to do. He then adopted the pattern that is most familiar in the home church. He went from house to house on repeated visits to win the trust of the people. "Gradually I got to know more families, old people who were lonely, busy mothers for whom I could do errands, foreign workers from Turkey who felt strange among their Christian neighbors. What I was doing was an example of the forty-day pioneer mission that prepares you for the eventual home church, which is a place where you live regularly."

Although he has been absent from this "experimental" village, and busy about church work in other parts of Germany, he keeps some contact with the neighborhood and says, "I still think of that as my own home church." Meanwhile, other German Unificationists have established home churches in their own neighborhood, especially those who are now lay associates, have families and "outside" jobs. He is of the modest opinion that "we have not made as much progress in Germany as they did in Korea, and more recently in England, and maybe in America."

A Korean home church leader told us that he continues to get inspiration from Reverend Moon, who teaches his followers to live for others and to cherish family life. This leader has a full-time job in private industry as a section chief in a large local factory. With his wife and children he says that he "feels an obligation" to be concerned for the 360 families in his immediate neighborhood. Because of some local anti-Moonie prejudice, they did not at first reveal they are members of the Unification Church. But their friendliness and their "good deeds" were soon appreciated by many who began to inquire why they were doing these things. After two years of such service they were able to count only eleven families who had joined the church, but they insisted that the purpose of the home church was being fulfilled: to bring love and kindness and service to people in the name of God. They reported also that in the fall of 1981 there were 230 home churches in the city of Seoul alone, and that similar home churches had been set up all over the Republic of Korea.

In Korea itself the Unification Church has evolved more extensively than anywhere else in the world, but it is still a minority even among Korean Christians. Many Unificationists in the city of Seoul are not yet personally committed to the Home Church movement. As a matter of current practice they attend religious services on Sundays

—and sometimes on Wednesday evenings—at any one of the thirty Unification centers, each of which is under the direction of a "district leader." This means that in Korea a stable pattern of churchgoing has emerged among those Moonies who live at home with their families and hold conventional jobs in the larger society. Our assumption has to be that the 230 home churches in the city are promoted by individuals (or married couples) who regularly attend services at the centers.

We have no reliable statistics on the number of Unificationists who frequent the thirty district church centers in Seoul, although we have been assured that the number of Korean Moonie converts is steadily increasing. Let us assume that in each of the 230 home church areas a good rapport has been reached with all 360 households, and that each of these families averages five persons. The total number of people thus contacted through the Home Church movement still constitutes a small minority among the many million inhabitants of the capital city. It must be repeated that the purpose of home church is to serve the needs of neighbors, not to bring them into Unification membership.

The actual service that is given in home church varies according to the talent of the church members and the recognized needs of the households being served. Spontaneity and creativity are encouraged, but the pattern of activity is gradually becoming formalized. After the Barrytown seminarians returned from their forty-day experience in England and Scotland in the summer of 1978, the seminary introduced into its curriculum a field work course in the Home Church program. Each student takes this course for one semester and is assigned a location for Home Church in one of the nearby towns. In this experimental design the area households are divided into three segments, with each divinity student visiting 120 families. Probably more than other members of the church the theology students take seriously Reverend Moon's prediction: "It is impossible to erect the Kingdom of Heaven on earth without fulfilling the Home Church mission."[19]

Social Reform

The Unification Church has been called a "world-transforming" movement which extends its influence beyond the spiritual conversion and salvation of individuals.[20] The church's ideology is geared to a complete reformation of all socio-cultural institutions: education, politics, economics, and even recreation. The collective concern for the whole world population begins with personal purification and the spirituality of marriage and family life. Enthusiastic members give witness to prospective recruits who are invited to dinners, meetings, and the series of lectures explaining *Divine Principle*. The approach of the Home Church to the whole neighborhood delays this proselytizing activity and replaces it with a mission of service.[21] The material, social and psychological needs of the neighbors are met before any mention is made of religion. The primary intention, therefore, of the Home Church is not to increase the number of Unificationists, but to manifest God's love to fellow human beings.

The ideological progression to total world reform leads from personal piety to family renewal to the Home Church ministry in the neighborhood. The anticipated evolution of the Home Church as the starting place for complete restoration of society may compare to the development of the *communidades de base,* the grass-roots movement among South American Catholics, commonly referred to as the Basic Christian Community.[22] Three stages may be discerned in the evolution of these local communities: (a) the formation of religious subgroups intent upon prayer, gospel sharing and sacramental devotions; (b) the second step is the group performance of social tasks, mutual aid within the neighborhood, improving collective facilities; (c) this is to culminate in the raising of consciousness, or a civic awareness and a commitment to the reform of the larger society.

While the ultimate goal of societal transformations—to restore the world to God—may be quite similar in these two forms of grass-roots religious organizations, certain dissimilarities are evident. The first difference is that the basic Christian community exists only among the poor and oppressed members of the Catholic population, and is neither attractive to, nor intended for, the bourgeoisie of whatever religion. The Unificationist Home Church is intended ultimately to exist everywhere and to reach out to people of all religions (or none) and of all social classes. Their universality is limited, and their development is delayed, only by the finite numbers of Unificationists available for the task.

Another important difference is the reversal of the first two stages: prayer that leads to social service, as compared with social service that leads to prayer. The basic Christian community starts with members of the same religion who gather for religious worship, Bible study and prayer. Out of this comes a recognition that they have a moral right to be liberated from oppression, illiteracy, endemic illnesses, and they are motivated then to the second stage of mutual aid. The Unificationist Home Church begins at the second stage by immediately offering to alleviate the needs of families and households. The dedicated Moonie arrives as an individual to render service to any and all persons and families among the 360 households in the immediate neighborhood. If there then evolves a stage of increased religiosity and spirituality it must be seen as an indeliberate consequence of the Moonies' selfless altruism.

The third stage of development in both approaches is the achievement of a better society, but the emphasis within the basic Christian community is on a group commitment, while in the Unificationist Home Church the emphasis tends to be on individualistic commitment. The Moonie doctrine is quite clear that personal reform is an absolute condition for social reform. No permanent change or improvement of the larger social structures and cultural institutions is thinkable unless the people have first been converted. It is a dictum also among the religious fundamentalists that the primary condition for a better society is the multiplication of born-again Christians.[23] Only when hearts and minds and behavior have been turned to God can we expect significant world transformation. The doctrine of the *Communidades* provides a contrasting view: the assurance that social reform can occur even before the citizenry has attained sanctity. On the other hand, a pious population may well continue to live in the midst of unworkable structures and oppressive institutions.

The programs of social reform at the grass-roots level differ significantly according to their respective views on Marxism. The Unificationists are so adamantly opposed to atheistic, materialistic communism that they repudiate the analytical methods proposed by the father of communism. The very concept of class struggle is seen as a Satanic attack on the capitalist system. The members of the basic Christian community in South America, however, are the poor and the underprivileged, now gradually becoming aware of their status as the working class. This awareness allows them to "accept Marxism as a tool, as a method of scientific analysis of reality that enables us to analyze the mechanisms by which a society evolves. . . . Understood in this way, Marxism is already, to a large extent, part of our present culture; it has in particular been adopted by the social sciences."[24] Even this analytical tool is anathema to the Moonies. Even where they promote the home church among the proletariat they are not likely to encourage any radical expression of class consciousness.

Social Welfare

The Unificationists who told us about their experiences in serving 360 households in a specific area spoke frequently of *my* Home Church, an indication that this ministry was assumed as a personal vocation. The designation of each specific home church is not the result of a mandate "from above," from New York headquarters, or from the state director of the church. The prime responsibility rests with the individual fully dedicated Moonie who has had wide experience encountering strangers in fund-raising and witnessing. "You go from door to door and tell the people you're a church missionary with a program of service to the community. We volunteer to help in their home if they need yard work, or small repairs, or housecleaning, or transportation for the elderly to go to the doctor, or to the store. We have a pickup truck to haul trash for them and a lawn mower to cut their grass." In actual practice the work of the home church is often taken as a joint responsibility of several members instead of a single individual.

The pattern of volunteer service, widely practiced in the American society, is almost always in affiliation with an organization like Red Cross, the St. Vincent de Paul Society, a hospital auxiliary, the United Way, where the individual cooperates with fellow volunteers in representing a well-known community fund drive. In the Home Church the Moonie volunteers to give service to complete strangers. I asked a center leader whether people are suspicious in meeting them and their offer of help.[25] He said that "at first they are reluctant to take help from a stranger. You actually have to develop a friendly relationship before they even let you help. Either they are suspicious of strangers or they have a feeling of pride that they can take care of themselves and their own needs. Once in a while some people want to take advantage of the church member and want you to come three hours a day, twice a week. I have to stress to the Home Church members that they might have to set a time limit to the service they can give to any one household."

When the older core member settles permanently in a fixed residential area—which is becoming increasingly frequent as married Moonies establish their own families—volunteer participation tends to become more organized. New lay associates are influenced by their good example: volunteers help to supervise playground activities, give instructions to retarded children, encourage teenagers to clean the streets and sidewalks of the neighborhood. In one Home Church area the members held a drive to collect newspapers and aluminum cans for recycling; in December they collected and donated canned goods to the local food bank for emergencies. In another area they organized a musical group that provided entertainment on various occasions in the neighborhood. It is sometimes difficult to distinguish whether the sponsorship of an activity is that of a home church leader or of the Unification urban center. In the one case it is the responsibility of an individual Moonie, and in the other it is a group responsibility.

In some of the larger cities where the numbers of lay associates have grown rapidly, the Unification centers and home churches cooperate ecumenically in the National Council for Church and Social Action. Distribution of food to the poor and hungry becomes a regular program where the members gather fresh produce from the city markets and distribute it at cost. Transportation is provided for the elderly; also programs for the protection of citizens against juvenile crime, as well as for the rehabilitation of juvenile delinquents. One Moonie activist who had majored in social work at college remarks that "home church is a fulfillment of both religion and social work."[26]

The dedicated service of the individual Moonie to the residents in the Home Church area logically evolves into cooperative efforts with other persons and other groups. The individual alone cannot complete the close spiritual relationship with God the Father because in the providence of God the person cannot be isolated from other human beings. The Christian notion of a community of saints places also an emphasis on the horizontal relationship of one person to another. The dedicated Moonie tells us that "salvation takes place within a community in a world of people who live together, not simply as individuals connected to God but also related to one another."[27]

Reverend Moon has deliberately clarified the primary purpose of the Home Church as loving service to humanity and not as the establishment of a house of worship, a parish or a congregation. The immediate task of social welfare and the broader development of social reform are involved in this demonstration of love and service on the part of the Moonie, for the non-Moonie. All of these activities are ultimately a means of bringing people closer to God. One may view this from the perspective of the missionary who is fulfilling a divine vocation of evangelization to the unsaved, but whose missionary goal has been focused on the mundane task of serving the needs of strangers. The task does not stop here. The Moonie vision encompasses a God-centered home church linked with all other home churches that reflect the restoration of the Kingdom of Heaven on earth.

The Family Model

From a structural perspective we are free to conclude that the home church is an alternative to the conventional parish or congregation, but it is not an alternative to the blessed family. In one of our interviews, Reverend Moon was quoted as saying that "home church is our destiny. It is not a witnessing technique like reaching people on the street or inviting them to a meal or a lecture. The home church is much deeper than this because it is integral to the building of God's Kingdom on earth. If there had been no sin in the Garden of Eden, if Adam and Eve had not fallen, theirs would have been the first home church. They would have grown to perfection with God as partner of their marriage and family. As their children multiplied into a tribe and then into a nation every God-centered family would have been a home church."

Focusing on the home church as a unit of sociological analysis—as we have done in these pages—could lead to the erroneous conclusion that it may exist in isolation from the total Unification Church. It is essential to realize that in the Unificationist conceptual framework the religious collectivity itself is a family, and that the main channel for the restoration of sinful humanity to God is the family. The Moonies want to use the terms "family" and "church" interchangeably. They like their church to be known as the "Unified Family," in which Reverend Moon and his wife are the "True Parents" of the members who are spiritual children. The church is the family, and the family is the church, but the Unification movement has not yet evolved to the point where the home church can be seen as family-type social unit.

At the present time in Europe and the United States, and to some extent also in Japan and Korea, the Moonies experience primary familial relationships only in the specific communities where the full-time members reside. Spiritual siblings, fully committed sisters and brothers, recognize each other as children in the God-centered Unification family. When the pastor of a Catholic territorial parish says that "we are a big happy family," he is speaking in hyperbole, suggesting that the loving primary relations of the ideal family are imitated by the parishioners. The Moonie in the typical urban center of the church wants the group to be much more than hyperbole, because the basic theme of personal salvation is through the family.

The ultimate goal of God's creation rests on the four-position foundation, manifested as "God, husband and wife, and their children."[28]

The typical Unification center where the core members live and out of which they carry on their full-time vocation is not the basic model for the home church. It is in some ways similar to the urban center where Franciscan friars live in community and minister to the needs of the faithful, most of whom are strangers to them. The Moonie center also provides lectures, distributes literature and conducts religious services. Like the Franciscans, the full-fledged Moonies share their lives, their tasks and their belongings, and address each other as members of the same family. Reverend Moon foresees that "in the future, our organization will become completely home church. National leaders, center leaders—everyone—will do home church work. Thus, the era of mobile activity will draw to a close, and everyone will settle down."[29]

In looking at the structural development of the Unification Church, it seems important to note that Reverend Moon does not talk of plans to organize parishes, dioceses, judicatories, or vicariates. "I emphasize that our movement has always been centered upon families as the basic unit of heavenly society. The family emphasis is always the same. This means that more blessings in marriage will be given, more children will be born, more families will be created. Then we will become elevated from the present communal type of centers to family-oriented homes. The family will always be the basic unit of happiness and cornerstone of the Kingdom of God on earth and thereafter in heaven."[30]

In the final analysis, the Home Church should probably be accepted as a manifestation of the divine program that Reverend Moon sees in evolution throughout all history, a restoration of humanity "with all the races standing side by side as brothers centered on Christ, who is the nucleus of Christianity. What makes Christianity different from other religions is that its purpose is to restore the one great world family which God had intended at the creation. This is to be accomplished by finding the True Parents of mankind through whom all men can become children of goodness through rebirth."[31]

The sense of urgency with which Unificationists serve non-members through the Home Church is built on the conviction that all will eventually be welcomed into God's "one great world family."

Footnotes

1 See the "Critique of the Theology of the Unification Church," pp. 103-118, in Irving Horowitz, ed., *Science, Sin and Scholarship,* Cambridge, MIT Press, 1978

2 Jaime Sheeran, "Evangelism and Witnessing," pp. 94-99, in Richard Quebedeaux, ed., *Lifestyle,* New York, Rose of Sharon Press, 1982

3 For example, see Joseph H. Fichter, "Hammering the Heretics: Religion vs. Cults," *The Witness,* vol. 66, no. 1, January 1983, pp. 4-6

4 For the description of modal parishioner, see Joseph H. Fichter, *Social Relations in the Urban Parish,* University of Chicago Press, 1954, chapter 4, "Social Solidarity and Modal Parishioners"

5 Eileen Barker, "Who'd Be a Moonie?" pp. 59-96, in Bryan Wilson, ed., *The Social Impact of New Religious Movements,* New York, Rose of Sharon Press, 1981

6 Remark of Unitarian minister George Exoo, p. 306, in Darrol Bryant, ed., *Proceedings* of Virgin Islands Seminar, New York, Rose of Sharon Press, 1980

7 Michael L. Mickler, "Crisis of Single Adults: An Alternative Approach," pp. 161-173, in Gene G. James, ed., *The Family and the Unificiation Church,* New York, Rose of Sharon Press, 1983

8 Barker, *op. cit.,* p. 93

9 In 1965 Reverend Moon blessed "holy ground" in 120 locations around the world, where his followers may visit to pray and meditate. See Neil Salonen, "History of the Unification Church," pp. 163-183, in Richard Quebedeaux, ed., *Lifestyle,* New York, Rose of Sharon Press, 1982

10 Joseph H. Fichter, "Conceptualization of the Urban Church," *Social Forces,* vol. 31, no. 1, October 1952, pp. 43-46

11 See Gibson Winter, *The Suburban Captivity of the Churches,* New York, Macmillan, 1962

12 Vatican II, "Constitution on the Sacred Liturgy," article 42

13 These are called "alternatives to established society," by Rosabeth Moss Kanter, *Commitment and Community,* Cambridge, Harvard University Press, 1972, p. vii

14 See Marguerite Bouvard, *The Intentional Community,* Port Washington, Kenikat Press, 1975; also Margaret Poloma, "Christian Covenant Communities," pp. 609-630, in Charles De Santo, *et al.,* eds., *A Reader in Sociology,* Scottsdale, Herald Press, 1980

15 Discussed by F.V. Filson, "The Significance of the Early House Churches," *Journal of Biblical Literature,* vol. lviii, 1939, pp. 105-112; see also Robert Banks, *Paul's Idea of Community: The Early House Churches in Their Historical Setting,* Grand Rapids, Eerdmans, 1980

16   Reported in *Time,* October 19, 1981, p. 109. Destructive persecution of the Unification Church in Brazil has also been reported in the news media. See Kenneth Freed, "Moonies Met by Mobs, Hostile Officials, in Tolerant Brazil," *Los Angeles Times,* September 8, 1981

17   Dan G. Fefferman, "CARP and Home Church," *Global Insight,* vol. 1, no. 1, January 1982, pp. 18-19

18   The concept of "restoration through indemnity" is found in *Divine Principle,* pp. 222-227, and is discussed by Young Oon Kim, *Unification Theology,* New York, Holy Spirit Association, 1980, pp. 229-233

19   See "Father's Explanation of Home Church," *Today's World,* September 1981, pp. 4-16

20   This theme is discussed by Anson Shupe and David Bromley, "Characteristics of World-Transformation Movements," *Sociological Analysis,* vol. 40, no. 4, Winter 1979, pp. 326-328

21   The advice of Reverend Won Pil Kim is: "You might think that you can change people with your wisdom and knowledge, but the only way change will happen is through sacrificial love." *Today's World,* vol. 2, no. 9, September 1981, p. 29

22   Gottfried Deelen, "The Church on Its Way to the People: Basic Christian Communities in Brazil," *Cross Currents,* vol. xxx, no. 4, Winter 1980-81, pp. 385-419. Basic communities were twice the theme of *Pro Mundi Vita Bulletin,* July 1976 and April 1980

23   See the treatment of "Fundamentalism as a Social Movement," pp. 227-258, in H. Paul Chalfant, Robert E. Beckley, C. Eddie Palmer, *Religion in Contemporary Society,* Sherman Oaks, Alfred Publishing, 1981

24   Deelen, *op. cit.,* p. 405, quoting Bishop Marcelo Cavalheira of Joao Pessoa

25   Unificationists in Northern New Jersey are welcomed by the elderly whose homes they clean, but the otherwise favorable news report was headlined "Moonies Get Their Foot in the Door," *Bergen Record,* June 22, 1981

26   Jamie Sheeran, p. 95, in Richard Quebedeaux (ed.), *Lifestyle,* New York, Rose of Sharon Press, 1982. See also Mose Durst, *To Bigotry, No Sanction,* Chicago, Regnery, 1984, "Creative Community Project," pp. 103-106

27   Anthony Guerra, quoted in Darrol Bryant, ed., *Proceedings* of the Virgin Islands Seminar, New York, Rose of Sharon Press, 1980, p. 175

28   *Divine Principle,* p. 32

29   See *Today's World,* vol. 2, no. 9, September 1981, p. 16

30   As told to Frederick Sontag, *Sun Myung Moon and the Unification Church,* Nashville, Abingdon, 1977, p. 157

31   *Divine Principle,* p. 123

VIII Moonies Against the Tide

One does not have to be a social scientist to note that we live in a rapidly changing society, but it is not clear to everyone that major institutions are changing at different rates of rapidity. In fact, it is sometimes inferred by sociologists that religion and family, because they change slowly, are a "drag" on the general direction and tempo of change. They continue to represent the "culture lag" that William Ogburn used to discuss. Even now it is argued that religions and families share a "set of values that sets them against the tide of the prevailing values in American society," with its focus on achievement, efficiency and competitiveness. The basic contemporary social value is said to be an emphasis on individualism and this "runs counter to the collectivist values underlying families and religions."[1]

The ecclesial-familial ideology of the Unification Church offers an opportunity to analyze the combined thrust of religion and family in resisting social change in the major institutions of the American society. In what ways is the Unification Church going "against the tide" of the onrushing modernization of the socio-cultural system? The central question of this chapter asks whether the Moonie adherence to traditional behavior patterns of marriage and family necessarily implies out-of-date values in the economic and political systems, in education and recreation. The Unification Church is largely counter-cultural, but it does not isolate itself from the world that it sees in need of moral reform. In an important speech in 1976, Reverend Moon declared that "the well-being of the family should come before that of the individual; the nation should come before the family; and the world before the nation and God before the world. This is the philosophy of the selfless way of life."[2] The ultimate Moonie goal is nothing short of the unification of all people in the Kingdom of God.

131

In the rough order of their importance in the Unificationist ideology, the topics we discuss here are illustrative of behavioral areas in which the Moonies run counter to contemporary trends. The most notable are those which guide the relations between male and female members. The central Moonie virtue is chastity, both before and during marriage. The fact that marriages are "arranged" by Reverend Moon is widely attacked as a most un-American system. Conditions must be met by the spouses before they are permitted to consummate their marriage and begin to have children. The status of women follows the Korean and Confucian ethic in contradiction to the contemporary feminist liberation movement.

Aside from the principles that regulate the male-female relationship, the Unificationist system of morality contravenes the ethic of conspicuous consumption and self-indulgence. Hard work and service to others offset the typical profit motive. The Moonies recognize sin as an offense against the heavenly Father and as a kind of alliance with Satan. They believe that their present behavior, or misbehavior, has an influence on the prospective Kingdom of God on earth.

The ecclesial system of the Unification movement is also in some ways out of step with the contemporary practices of Christian churches. To centralize sacramentality on the one experience of the holy wine ceremony is the abandonment of the long and revered Christian tradition of sacraments. The induction of new members is a combination of emotional persuasion and intellectual indoctrination that raises a storm of protest by the church's critics who label it "brainwashing." Membership in the Unification Church is also different from that of the relatively exclusivistic practices of most Christian denominations. The Moonie may attend worship services at any other church and even claim to continue membership in the previous church affiliation.

Vocation to Chastity

It appears that the large, mainline religions in the west have failed to "stem the tide" of increasing premarital and extramarital sexuality. Sociologists see this wave of permissiveness as a product of contemporary social structures and values. In some instances the churches too have "relaxed" their values and doctrines to accommodate the behavior patterns and preferences of their adherents. The Unification Church, on the contrary, has determinedly withstood this evolution and with remarkable tenacity insists on premarital celibacy and chaste marital fidelity. The *Divine Principle* attributes the "Fall of Man," the sinful nature of the human race, to the act of fornication between Eve and the Archangel. All human misery in the world is in some way a consequence of that original sin of illicit sex. "In present conditions no one can prevent the crime of adultery, which has become increasingly prevalent as the development of civilization makes human life easier and more indolent."[3]

The young recruits to the Unification Church understand from the beginning that premarital sexual relations are absolutely forbidden. They must deliberately avoid "romantic attachments" and must learn to develop familial relations of spiritual siblings across gender lines. As children of God and of their true parents, Mr. and Mrs. Moon, they work and pray and play together as brothers and sisters. The strength of moral character thus achieved is the basis of a spiritual relationship with God, the Father, but it is also preparatory to their own future parenthood.

"When a Unification Church member is single and new to the church, he does many things—fund-raising, witnessing, working in church businesses, studying theology. From a Unification perspective, however, these are secondary to what's happening within him internally. Moonies are trying to become true people—true sons and daughters of God in order to become ideal as husbands and wives and parents. This effort is fundamental to the Unification way of life."[4] Self-control and self-denial in the area of sex relations are characteristic of the unselfishness the Moonies try to develop in all areas of social relations. Their filial relation with God the Father is constantly expressed in their selfless fraternal relations with other people. The life of chastity is a social as well as a personal commitment.

Marital fidelity is an absolute requirement for the Moonie married couple. The theology of restoration and of redemption arises from the historical fact that human friendship with God, the Father, was disrupted by the original sin of illicit sex. The implication is that salvation necessarily begins with the avoidance of fornication before marriage and of adultery during marriage. Marital fidelity means not only an avoidance of extramarital sexual relations, but also the avoidance of divorce. Since the second blessing at the wine ceremony is a "mandate from heaven," it is a permanent unbreakable bond. The Moonie spouse who deserts, separates, or obtains a divorce is immediately excluded from the Unificationist fellowship. The innocent spouse who remains faithful is free to accept another matching.

These principles of fidelity between husband and wife have lost their moral influence on a high proportion of married Americans. The large number of divorces reported annually is clear evidence that the Moonie ideals of marital permanence and stability constitute a countercultural trend. The prohibition against divorce was once traditional in organized religion in America, but gradual concessions have been made for permissable divorce (and remarriage) under certain conditions. It is likely that most divorced people had honestly intended at the time of their wedding to keep their marriage vows and to persevere in a lasting marriage. The fact is, of course, that the divorce rates have soared to unprecedented numbers, even among churchgoers. To the extent, however, that the Moonie couples persevere in chaste marriages they represent an outstanding countercultural trend. The careful preparation for marriage, and the theological principles on which those preparations rest, are deeply serious motivations to "stem the tide" of broken marriages and disrupted families.

Mate Selection

Nothing could be more un-American than a prearranged marriage. In the typical American pattern of boy-girl dating the period of courtship (if that word is still used) culminates in the decision to become "engaged," but among the Moonies the engagement, or "matching," is the beginning of courtship. In a more accurate sense, the prearranged matching of future spouses precludes both courtship and engagement. The process that has evolved in the church begins when a marriageable Unificationist, who has reached the mid-twenties and has been a church member for at least three years, submits a simple application form, which is then studied by the Blessing Committee composed of older Blessed wives. "They gather information for Reverend Moon on members eligible for the Blessing."[5]

The slogan that "marriages are made in heaven" is not taken seriously by even the most romantic American youth, but it is a matter of religious faith among the Moonies. The concept of romantic love as a reason for getting married is repudiated among them. The true believer is sure that God has preordained the ideal spouse for each church member. One happily married couple said that this gave them a greater feeling of security than relying on themselves. "We felt that our marriage was chosen in heaven. It was decided by God, not by us—although we participated in that decision through our consent." Since marriage is the only genuine life vocation open to the faithful Unificationist, the ceremony of selecting one's life mate is an occasion of great excitement.

The large numbers of marriage candidates who assemble on the date and place appointed for the matching ceremony have confidence that their Father Moon is divinely inspired and guided in the choices he makes. Each couple, upon being designated by their spiritual leader, is asked to leave the assembly for a brief private conversation during which they decide whether or not to accept this commitment. The great majority of couples return to the assembly in the conviction that God's will for their marriage has been expressed to them through the prayerful judgment of his earthly representative. The wine ceremony fixes a perpetual bond, a new lineage, between them, but they must wait for permission to consummate their union. Nor do they "set the date" for the large public mass wedding, the actual blessing ceremony, which may be postponed for as long as three years. This decision also is made for them by their spiritual father, Reverend Moon. This period of waiting, however, is neither an engagement nor a courtship.

The brother-sister relationship which existed for each couple before the matching shifts now to the prospective husband-wife relationship, but they neither live together nor work together. They may be assigned to missions at some distance from each other in this country, or even in different foreign countries. Instead of the almost constant companionship experienced by the typical young American engaged couple, the matched Moonies are subjected to the "test" of distance in the recognition that their prospective married life is more than strong personal love and romantic attachment. This period of separation therefore involves only occasional personal contact and some communication by letter and telephone. The length of the waiting period has varied in the past but almost always ends with a mass wedding.[6] The couples who were matched at the World Mission Center in New York in May 1979 were finally publicly married three years later at the mass ceremonial wedding at Madison Square Garden in July 1982. Most of them had already been civilly married immediately following the wine ceremony, but even now after the public wedding they would not yet live together as husband and wife.

Delayed Parentage

The divinely ordained vocation of every Unificationist is marriage and parenthood, which is seen as the fulfillment of God's plan for the human race, both personally and collectively. This is a serious moral obligation, not to be ignored or lightly assumed. It parallels the sacred duty of Jewish religion where "to marry and establish a family is a *mitzvah,* a religious commandment."[7] Preparation for marriage presupposes that several years' membership in the church have resulted in the "first blessing" in which the individual attains a close loving relationship with God. This is a spiritual preparation for all of one's life, but it is specially relevant as a precondition for marriage, which is the second and principal blessing.

The so-called Blessing "Tribe" to which each couple is assigned is available also for consultation and advice all during the engagement period. Their central concern is to assure that the couple is properly prepared for marriage and that they are able to handle the responsibilities of children and family. They start with the assumption that members who have been dedicated to the church's values and work and have remained celibate for at least three years are willing to prepare conscientiously for marriage. Also, the deliberate delay of three years is a lengthy waiting period even for spiritually dedicated young people who are in love. The physical separation while they carry out individual missions often constitutes problems that they now discuss with the central figure of the Blessing Tribe.[8] It is likewise from this person, always a man, that they must obtain permission finally to consummate the marriage.

The beginning of the family, or the consummation of the marriage, is typically delayed for forty days after the public mass wedding. This is generally regarded as an "absolute condition" for the spiritual foundation for the God-centered family. "We liken it to Jesus fasting in the wilderness for forty days prior to beginning his public ministry." On one exceptional occasion, the spouses who were joined at the mass wedding of 700 couples in 1975 were asked to maintain sexual continence and to delay their actual married life for a period of three years while they were sent out separately on the mission of worldwide evangelization. From a secular and rational perspective this postponement appears to be a hindrance to the dvelopment of marital affection, but the Moonies accept it as a sacrifice of indemnity and as a contribution to the Father's divine plan of salvation.

Reverend Moon encourages his followers to have children, but it is doubtful if any of them aspire to have as large a family as he and Mrs. Moon have produced. There is no official church teaching about contraceptive means of birth control, and the spouses say they are free to make their own decisions in this area. Nevertheless, abstinence from marital relations, like fasting from food, is occasionally observed as a spiritual condition of indemnity. While statistics on the birthrate of American Moonies are not yet available, the general attitude expressed among married members is that four children are considered a "large family." Most of the Unification women are in their late twenties, or early thirties, before they begin to have children.

To the extent that this delayed parentage results in relatively small families the Moonies may be said to conform to the general American pattern of fewer children. On the other hand, the practice of celibacy during the engagement period and for some time into the marriage itself is clearly contrary to the typical American pattern of early and frequent sexual intercourse.

The Status of Women

The earliest Korean converts to the Unification religion were mainly women and for about a decade, even in Europe and America, the membership remained largely female. The first Unification missionary from Korea to the United States was a woman, their leading theologian, Young Oon Kim. The academic dean of the Barrytown Seminary is a woman who encourages female Moonies to study there as well as at other graduate schools of divinity. Most of the itinerant workers are women, and many are captains of mobile fund-raising teams. Among the 49 teams, however, active in the International One World Crusade in 1983, only three were headed by women.[9]

As the sex ratio of the membership shifted to a male majority, there occurred a kind of Koreanization of the relationship between the Unificationist brothers and sisters. The church in America has not completely escaped the influence of the Confucian and Korean ideology of female submissiveness and male assertiveness. The important administrative posts at the New York headquarters are mainly in the hands of men, yet a discernible contrast appears between the ecclesial and the familial institutions. In Europe and America, if not in Japan and Korea, the ecclesial role of women tends toward egalitarianism.[10] Yet, the familial role tends toward the "feminine mystique" when the Moonie mother settles down to the raising of children.

The central question at this point is the extent to which the Moonie women differ from the contemporary trend toward women's liberation. It is clear from both theory and practice that the so-called sexual revolution, allowing an increase of promiscuity in the female population, is entirely contrary to the Unification ideology. The other aspect of women's liberation, which allows choice and demands responsibility, is clearly exhibited among the devoted female members. The *Divine Principle* does teach the equality of human beings across sex lines, but there are fixed cultural roles that are difficult to upset. Where the community is large, as in New York, the patterns seem to exhibit that the sisters do the cooking and the laundry, while the men are engaged in "more important" tasks.

One of the feminist complaints among the mainline Christian churches is the patriarchal tradition according to which only the male ministers are able to exercise a kind of paternalistic authority in a hierarchical system. There are no ordained clergy in the Unification Church, so that the demand for women's ordination is never raised. Informally, about twenty Korean and European men have the title of "Reverend," but no women. The fact that Unificationist theology focuses strongly on God, the Father, whose heart is pained by the sins of his children and who demands a full measure of devotion and adoration, greatly influences an appreciation of human fatherhood. One never hears of the "motherhood" of God among the Moonies.[17] Reverend Moon, the founder of the church, is often fondly called "Father" and he and Mrs. Moon are regarded as the "True Parents," but I have never heard her called "Mother" Moon.

It seems important also to note that Reverend Moon plays the role of "double paternity" in the process of matchmaking of prospective spouses. In the traditional system of arranged marriages, common not only in Asiatic countries but over most of the ancient world, the father of the bride consults with the father of the groom and they come to a satisfactory agreement about the forthcoming nuptials. In the Unification Church Reverend Moon acts in the capacity of father for both spouses, and under divine inspiration he blesses the espousal. This powerful spiritual influence tends to reinforce paternal authority.

Puritan Ethic

The so-called Calvinist ethic of hard work, frugality, constraint and "this-worldly" asceticism, is apparent in the behavior of Moonies. They favor a "dress code" of modest clothing for women and coat-and-tie attire for males, who are not to have beards or long hair. They are severely criticised, and often harassed, for their mendicant practice of "fund-raising" by selling flowers and soliciting money for various good causes on street corners and at airports. The fact is that funds are raised also through the hard work of groups operating a fishing enterprise, a restaurant, a janitorial service, a vegetable farm, and other enterprises.[12] A third source of income is the more conventional church practice of tithing. Lawyers, professors, business men and women, and other members in various occupations give their salaries to the local Moonie community in which they are living. As more blessed couples set up their own homes and establish families they continue to donate generously to the church coffers.

Although they feel no shame in imitating the medieval pattern of mendicancy they do not intend to imitate the life of poverty of Saint Francis of Assisi. While they readily share their goods with fellow Moonies they do not pronounce a vow of religious poverty. When they work among the poor and needy they have no intention of adopting for themselves the lifestyle of the poor. Their intention is to do all they can to alleviate poverty and to help raise families out of their poverty. They make it clear that the old-fashioned virtues of diligence and thrift are essential for upward mobility. They are generous to the underprivileged, the unfortunate and the needy, but their efforts are directed to the development of individual competence that can help raise poor families out of their deprived status.

The fact that they share their own belongings with fellow members of the church, and also contribute to the alleviation of families in need, exemplifies their belief in a more equitable distribution of the world's goods. The "Day of All Things" is one of the four annual holy days celebrated by the Unificationists, and it is in reference to God's dominance over all the world. This is the third Blessing achieved by mankind which evolves from the first (unite with God) and the second (unite with each other) Blessings. It seems correct to say that although Reverend Moon abhors communism, his teachings may easily lead to a kind of beneficial economic socialism.

The Puritan spirit is exhibited in some behavior patterns and not in others. For example, they express their spiritual joy in group dancing, music and singing, and in the dramatic arts generally. On the other hand, they show moderation in eating and drinking, especially in the use of alcoholic beverages. While they are not doctrinaire prohibitionists, they recognize the social and personal evils of alcoholism and drug abuse. Their abstemious behavior may be seen as an example of the moral self-control of the virtuous person, and an example of the moral counter-culture, quite contrary to the youthful notion of "letting it all hang out."

Sin and Satan

It is the teaching of *Divine Principle* that when Eve committed the original human sin, the angel who seduced her became Satan. "The angel fell as the result of an immoral act of unnatural lust, and that act was fornication." What happened in the early Paradise was to have profound and negative effects on all human beings who descended from the first parents, Adam and Eve. The Unificationists accept the word from their scripture that "the original sin is transmitted from generation to generation. Every religion which teaches how to eliminate sin has called adultery the greatest sin, and has emphasized an ascetic life in order to prevent it."[13] Satan seems to have disappeared from the vocabulary of most mainline preachers. "For many modern men, the doctrines of original sin, inherited guilt and total depravity are impossible to believe because they seem both unreasonable and immoral."[14]

Since sin is a grave offense against God and brings pain to the heart of the loving Father, it is considered a form of Satanic behavior. The Unificationist is surrounded by a materialistic world in which evil spirits abound. People who oppose Reverend Moon and who attack the church are representatives of Satan. They tempt the members to leave the church and this is why the members are often told to look upon their relatives and friends who urge them to leave as minions of the Devil. The road to salvation is threatened by multitudes of evil spirits who are trying to draw the members into sin and away from God and the church.

The doctrine of the "Fall" is accepted by the Moonies as the main explanation of human sinfulness, and the individual who now commits personal sin has done so by forming a "reciprocal base with Satan." This does not mean that human freedom and responsibility have been usurped by the dominance of the devil. Indeed, by contrast, the person who turns away from sin to practice virtue does so by forming a "reciprocal basis with God," instead of with Satan.[15] The power of Satan, however, must be taken seriously because "the objects of Satan are the evil spirits in the spirit world." Belief in the actual existence of a personal devil, which is strongly held among the Unificationists, appears to have lost its hold on the majority of secularized Americans. As in other aspects of religion the Moonies are here again going "against the tide."

When Menninger asked *Whatever Became of Sin?* he was concerned about the absence of guilt feelings among sinners, as well as by the general lack of responsibility in choosing between right and wrong. The Moonie, on the other hand, has a keen sense that "sin is the act of violating the heavenly law," and that the "pangs of conscience" will afflict the person who victimizes his neighbor. The new world envisioned by Reverend Moon "will usher in a new age when the sinful history of mankind has been liquidated. It must be a world in which no sin is possible." If we could "feel the presence of God and know the heavenly law that sinners are sent to hell, who then would dare to commit sin?"[16]

Approaching the End Time

Religious fundamentalists and Pentecostals frequently issue dire warnings about the approaching end of time, but most Americans seem uninterested in such predictions (with the exception of those who fear a nuclear holocaust). There is an urgency about the Unification program of personal salvation because humanity is moving toward the imminent establishment of the Kingdom of God on earth. Not much time is left in these "last days" to develop God-centered families, populate the earth with blessed children, and transform the socio-political order. According to Unificationist teaching we are already in "the day of the Lord's Second Coming," and have a moral obligation to cooperate in the divine mission.

This is not in anticipation of a dreadful apocalypse, a destructive Armageddon, a harsh final judgment, because "Unification theology looks at the age to come as a time of fulfilled hope and intense joy."[17] As a factor of personal effort and social progress, the eschatological optimism of the Moonies has never permitted their church to become a "doomsday cult," as John Lofland originally dubbed it. On the contrary, they confidently look forward to an age of glory when all humanity will be caught up in the third and eternal blessing, which is God's complete dominion over all things. All creation—even the world of evil spirits—will be united in the loving embrace of the divine Father.

In contrast to the millions of people who express a genuine fear that humanity is now on the verge of massive self-destruction, with the threat of ever-proliferating lethal weapons, the Unificationists demonstrate an optimistic faith in the restoration of all things in God. They are sure that we are currently already in the messianic age, the time of the "Second Coming," but they realize that tremendous efforts must still be made in purifying human relations. The divine will may not be fulfilled till God-centered families multiply and expand to a God-centered world. This is seen as an enormous enterprise to which every person must contribute.

There appears to be uncertainty in the minds of interviewed Unificationists about the place of the Second Coming and about the exact time of the Advent. Nevertheless, they cheerfully say that "the new age will see one world, one kingdom; through God's direct guidance, goodness will steadily rise and evil will eventually decline."[18] In their first enthusiasm some young Moonies are sure that this new age will occur within their lifetime, but their expectations gradually diminish over the passing years. The prophecy of the Second Advent says that "the nation of the East where Christ will come again would be none other than Korea."[19] Moonies believe that the one to come has already been announced. "With the fullness of time, God has sent His messenger to resolve the fundamental questions of life and the universe. His name is Sun Myung Moon."[26]

When the Unificationists take seriously the coming of the Kingdom of God they do not differ essentially from the general belief asserted by Christians over the centuries. This expectation is voiced every time a Christian recites the Lord's prayer, but it is estimated that about sixty percent actually believe in the Second Coming, and probably very few of them expect it to happen soon. While the Unification belief is shared by fundamentalists, it is most likely that they are going against the tide of popular belief.

Non-sacramental Church

One would expect that a church that focuses so closely on family life should celebrate rituals and sacraments that deliberately draw attention to family happenings. Traditional Christianity is ultimately related to the most significant events that occur in the generational development of the family. As Moberg writes, "Life-cycle rituals help to cushion shock, carry people over crises and symbolize passage from one stage of life to the other."[21] Organized religion tends to provide values and norms with which people meet their moral obligations at every period of life; it also introduces a sacred celebration for each. Similarly, "the Confucian *rites de passage* emphasize the importance of family consciousness and family loyalties in the life of an individual. They demonstrate the *familial* orientation of Confucian religious practice."[22]

In its sparse liturgy, and in its singular emphasis on the marriage blessing, the Unification Church has neglected both the ritual system of the Korean tradition and the practices of Western Christianity. Faithful observant Christians enter marriage with the sacrament, have their children baptized and confirmed. The traditional list of seven Christian sacraments includes also reconciliation, the Eucharist, holy orders, and the last rites. Although insisting that they be accepted as a Christian church, the Unificationists reject the whole sacramental system which has for centuries been a spiritual and moral support of the family system. The two Christian festivals, Christmas and Easter, that are occasions for family celebration, are not high on the Moonie liturgical calendar. Even the communion service, commemorating Christ's Last Supper in the symbolic gesture of community solidarity, has no place among the Moonie rituals. Little attention is paid to funeral rites, although they are sacred in oriental and Western religions. As one member remarked, "Though I imagine there are ceremonies surrounding death, I have not yet experienced them."[23]

The Unification liturgical calendar calls for group religious services on Sundays and the first day of every month, as well as on four special holy days in the year: Parents' Day, Children's Day, the Day of All Things, and God's Day. Perhaps the closest resemblance to a traditional Christian sacrament is the holy wine ceremony which seals the marriage agreement and also acts as a spiritual rebirth, liberating the soul from both personal and original sin. In lieu of baptism, or "christening," the parents dedicate the newborn child to God on the eighth day of life.[24] The most frequently repeated ritual in the life of the Moonie is the so-called "spiritual condition." We are told that "a condition is an offering an individual makes to God for a specific time period and reason. For instance, everyone in the church does a seven-day fast. This, much like baptism, represents dying to the fallen world and being reborn to God."[25]

Recruiting Spiritual Children

One of the qualifications for being matched is that the dedicated young Moonie must bring at least three "spiritual children" into the church.[26] In preparation for the sacred vocation of marriage and family life, the young member resembles the most zealous evangelicals in the fundamentalist religions by making converts. The two church functions in which all Unificationists participate are fund-raising and witnessing, and the latter means bringing the message of Reverend Moon's *Divine Principle* to anyone who will listen. The great majority of neophytes have been brought into the church through personal contact. The answer to the question "Where and how did you meet the church?" is almost invariably an encounter with a believing Moonie.

There is usually, however, a disclaimer that any pressure was put on the potential member. As though to contradict the stories about brainwashing and deception, we were told in one interview, "I wanted to correct them and to teach them more about religion than they knew." Another said, "Nobody ever tried to change my mind. I studied the *Divine Principle* and listened to the lectures. That's what convinced me they had the right answers." One of the ex-members remarked that Moon's ideas catch on effectively because they are relatively simple. "He is convinced that the Divine Principles are the most logical and most natural divine revelation that conclusively clarifies all the fundamental questions raised by the Bible."[27]

The weightiness of the religious arguments is apparently the central feature of the recruitment of new members, and their simplicity is satisfactory for those in doubt. An ex-Catholic young lady had her theological problems solved, for example, when she realized that Jesus was not meant to die as the will of God; she now understands the Trinity because it is God the Father to whom she must pray; she now has assurance that she can reach the state of perfection which eluded her as a Catholic. The salvific solution is in the Second Blessing. For the ordinary members of the Unification Church, once the *Divine Principle* has been accepted there need be no further attempt to understand the ongoing mysteries of Christianity.

As a Catholic priest, I am more than ordinarily interested in the reasons why some Catholics are attracted to the Unification Church. In answer to my usual question, one enthusiastic Moonie, who had spent years as a Franciscan sister, explained that she was first attracted by "the friendliness and personal concern they showed for each other and for me. In my religious life I had always had a close personal relationship with Jesus, but now I saw these people reaching out and embracing everyone in the universal love of God." When I replied that all this is contained also within Catholicism: "You understood the Mystical Body of Christ. You knew the social encyclicals since the time of Leo XIII," her simple response was kindly and to the point: "Yes, but the Moonies put all this into practice."

The earliest contact with the Unification community is not, therefore, the consequence of either a born-again experience or of a long search for the solution of spiritual and theological problems. Recruitment to the Moonies is then typical of modern youth movements—rather than of the mainline churches—in response to a kind of subjective search for self-actualization.[28] A gradual indoctrination in the teachings of *Divine Principle* is accompanied by the example of cheerful, healthy and concerned comradeship so that the young recruit is brought to the point of full acceptance of the church. Very quickly the neophyte is involved in one or another group activity, like the young man who met a member of the Creative Community Project in California. "I was invited up to this ranch where they did organic gardening. I was really into that whole idea of living with the land, in harmony with nature. After I went to the center at Berkeley I did notice a Bible or two. That interested me, but not enough to probe."

Multiple Membership

From the perspective of the Unification Church the new member is not required to repudiate allegiance to any other, and former, religious tradition. In this sense it is not in conflict with other churches, although most of the mainline churches would hardly reciprocate in officially "sharing" membership rolls with the Moonies. Another modern American "church," Scientology, also allows its members to attend other churches, but the notion of multiple religious participation seems peculiar to the Japanese, who do not make clear-cut distinctions among the several oriental religions. One may suggest that the Unification Church is very liberal and modern in allowing its members to continue their loyalties and even their affiliation in non-Moonie churches.

One of the veteran members, a woman of Catholic origins who had been a state director, points out that "the purpose of the Unification Church is to revitalize churches, to bring Christianity alive, to understand all world religions and to become part of all of them, rather than to become separate from all of them."[29] As an association dedicated to the task of Christian unity, it has no intention of replacing other denominations, or of becoming a super-church, or even of remaining in existence after all Christians have been united. One is reminded of the Disciples of Christ, originally introduced by Barton Stone and Thomas Campbell, whose "Christian movement" was meant to be both all-embracing and nondenominational. It is a species of exaggerated ecumenism that blurs the legitimate boundaries identifying denominational affiliation and suggests a religious indifference to the profession of faith.

There is no question, however, that the devout member has a fierce personal loyalty to the charismatic Sun Myung Moon, forms a close attachment to fellow Moonies, has a strong belief in the theological doctrines of the church, and a zealous dedication to the Unification mission of restoring all things to God, the Father. The important oddity in this apparently solidaristic membership is that it is not an exclusive community separating itself from all other denominations and churches. One young Moonie, an ex-Catholic who has been a member for seven years, assured me, "I didn't stop being a Catholic when I joined the Moonies. I go to mass and communion whenever I visit my family." Such persons are obviously ignorant of the membership requirements in the Catholic Church, but they are well aware that most Unificationists are quite willing to participate in any and all religious congregations.

It is still a common stereotype about the Moonies that their main immediate goal is to lure young people into the community where they overwhelm them with kindness, deceive them with false doctrines, and brainwash them into a kind of perpetual enslavement to the will of Reverend Moon. In other words, like the postulant to a Catholic religious order, the prospective Moonie quickly learns that eternal salvation depends upon a dedicated acceptance of the patterns of life in a closed community of strict rules and regulations. The outside world is full of materialistic people who do the work of evil spirits in drawing the neophyte away from this spiritual vocation.

Footnotes

1 "Families and Religions Beset by Friends and Foes," pp. 9-16, in William D'Antonio and Joan Aldous, eds., *Families and Religions: Conflict and Change in Modern Society,* Beverly Hills, Sage Publications, 1983
2 Keynote address at Yankee Stadium Rally, June 1, 1976
3 *Divine Principle,* p. 75
4 "Engagement, Marriage and Children," pp. 1-26, in Richard Quebedeaux, ed., *Lifestyle: Conversations with Members of the Unification Church,* New York, Rose of Sharon Press, 1982
5 *Ibid.,* p. 2
6 The rate of "attrition" of matched couples between the wine ceremony and the public wedding is estimated at about fifteen percent
7 Marshall Sklare, *America's Jews,* p. 74, New York, Random House, 1971
8 The precondition of gaining three converts, or spiritual children, before consummating a marriage may be waived for "older women" in their thirties
9 Listed in *Unification News,* vol. 2, no. 12, p. 6, December 1983
10 See the discussion on "Women's Caucus," pp. 113-124, in Richard Quebedeaux, ed., *Lifestyle,* New York, Rose of Sharon Press, 1982; also Elizabeth Clark, "Women in the Theology of the Unification Church," pp. 109-121, in M. Darrol Bryant and Susan Hodges, eds., *Exploring Unification Theology,* New York, Rose of Sharon Press, 1978
11 It is noted, however, that spiritual rebirth comes through "Jesus, the spiritual True Father, and the Holy Spirit, the spiritual True Mother," *Divine Principle,* p. 216
12 A list of socially concerned Moonie groups are described by Kurt Johnson, pp. 75-84, in Quebedeaux, ed., *Lifestyle*
13 *Divine Principle,* pp. 71, 75
14 Young Oon Kim, *Unification Theology,* New York, 1980, p. 90
15 For the connections among these various concepts see *Divine Principle,* pp. 83-95
16 *Ibid.,* p. 12
17 Young Oon Kim, *Unification Theology,* p. 223
18 Young Oon Kim, *Unification Theology and Christian Thought,* New York, Golden Gate, 1976 (revised edition), p. 293
19 *Divine Principle,* Chapter VI, "Second Advent," pp. 497-536
20 *Ibid.,* p. 16

21 David Moberg, *The Church as a Social Institution*, Englewood Cliffs, Prentice-Hall, 1962, p. 350

22 Julia Ching, *Confucianism and Christianity*, New York, 1977, p. 174

23 On the death of his son, Hueng-Jim, Reverend Moon said, "Let us not use the word funeral any longer, but let us call our services the Ascension and Harmony Celebration." See *Unification News*, January 1984, pp. 5, 19

24 Luke 2/21: "When eight days were fulfilled" Mary and Joseph named the child Jesus. See Quebedeaux, *Lifestyle*, p. 11

25 Patricia Zulkosky, "Piety and Spirituality," pp. 51-71, in Richard Quebedeaux, ed., *Lifestyle*, New York, Rose of Sharon Press, 1982

26 Some exceptions have been made in the case of older Moonies and of those in graduate doctoral studies

27 Klaus Lindner, "Kulturelle und Semantische Probleme," pp. 219-234, in Gunter Kehrer, ed., *Das Entstehen Einer Neuen Religion*, Munich, Kösel-Verlag, 1981

28 The earliest analyst of the Unification conversion process was John Lofland, "Becoming a World-Saver—Revisited," pp. 10-23, in James T. Richardson, ed., *Conversion Careers*, Beverly Hills, Sage, 1978

29 M. Darrol Bryant and Susan Hodges, eds., *Exploring Unification Theology*, New York, Rose of Sharon Press, 1978, p. 63. She says also, "I attend an Episcopal church every Sunday," p. 75

Index